THE LIBRARY OF
AMERICAN
LIVES AND TIMES™

FREDERICK DOUGLASS

From Slave to Statesman

Alice Fleming

The Rosen Publishing Group's
PowerPlus Books™
New York

Published in 2004 by The Rosen Publishing Group, Inc.
29 East 21st Street, New York, NY 10010

First Edition

Editor's Note: All quotations have been reproduced as they appeared in the letters and diaries from which they were borrowed. No correction was made to the inconsistent spelling that was common in that time period.

Library of Congress Cataloging-in-Publication Data

Fleming, Alice Mulcahey, 1928–
Frederick Douglass : from slave to statesman / Alice Fleming.
    p. cm. — (The library of American lives and times)
Summary: A biography of the runaway slave who became an abolitionist, an orator and writer, and a crusader for women's rights.
Includes bibliographical references and index.
ISBN 0-8239-6624-0 (lib. bdg.)
1. Douglass, Frederick, 1817?–1895—Juvenile literature. 2. African American abolitionists—Biography—Juvenile literature. 3. Abolitionists—United States—Biography—Juvenile literature. 4. Antislavery movements—United States—History—19th century—Juvenile literature. [1. Douglass, Frederick, 1817?–1895. 2. Slaves. 3. Abolitionists. 4. African Americans—Biography. 5. Antislavery movements.] I. Title. II. Series.
E449.D75 F57 2004
973.8'092—dc21

                    2002009507

Manufactured in the United States of America

CONTENTS

1. A Voice of Freedom

When Frederick Douglass was a fifteen-year-old slave, his master hired him out to a farmer named Edward Covey, who beat him almost every day. After six months of this abuse, Frederick rebelled. The next time that Covey seized him, Frederick fought back. The slave driver was powerless in the hands of the broad-shouldered teenager. No matter how hard Covey kicked and flailed, he could not break Frederick's grip. After several minutes, Frederick let Covey go, but not before announcing that he would not tolerate another beating. Covey was humiliated. He never laid a hand on Frederick again.

That incident was a turning point in Frederick Douglass's life. Once he found the courage to stand up to his abuser, he regained the self-respect and self-confidence that had been beaten out of him by slavery. He realized that, although someone else claimed to own his body, his spirit was his own.

Opposite: Frederick Douglass, photographed in the 1850s, wrote of his first months on Covey's farm, "I was broken in body, soul and spirit . . . the cheerful spark that lingered about my eye died; the dark night of slavery closed in upon me; and behold a man transformed into a brute!"

"I was a changed man after that fight," he wrote later. "I was nothing before. I WAS A MAN NOW."

In that moment, Frederick Douglass knew he could, and would, find a way to throw off the bonds of slavery and become a free man. He had already taught himself to read and write, and, as a free man, he would discover his gift for public speaking. His extraordinary voice and his mastery of the English language eventually won him international recognition. His books and newspaper articles added to his fame.

Frederick Douglass became a leader in the fight for the abolition of slavery and the struggle to win equal rights for blacks. At the time, few Americans cared about either issue. Slavery had been accepted in the American colonies since 1619, when the first slave ship from Africa arrived in Virginia. By the time Frederick Douglass was born, some 200 years later, the institution was so well established that even people who disliked it saw no hope of ending it. The U.S. Constitution defined slaves as property. Slaves who escaped to a free state could be captured as fugitives and returned to their masters. In most states, even free blacks were not allowed to vote, own property, or serve on juries.

In the beginning of the nineteenth century, the United States was divided along social, religious, and climatic lines. The free states were in the North, where farms were small, diversified to accommodate the changes in the seasons, and dependent on crops, such as corn, that were not labor intensive. The principal industries in the North were manufacturing and shipping. Slavery on a large scale had proved to be unnecessary in that part of the country. Society was different in the South, where the climate was milder and agriculture was the main industry. Land was cheap and plentiful, and cotton, tobacco, and other labor-intensive crops were grown on a few very large plantations and many more smaller farms. Owning slaves required a sizable initial investment, but proved profitable in the long run, as they provided cheap labor on these sprawling estates. Different social and religious institutions

Benjamin Henry Latrobe's 1798 watercolor shows slaves at work under the watchful eye of an overseer. Slavery, wrote essayist John Jay Chapman, was "a sleeping serpent" that "lay coiled up under the table" of American politics from the first days of the Constitutional Convention. It was preparing to strike and divide the nation in two.

developed around the urban centers of the North and the isolated, self-sufficient farms of the South.

These differences between the North and the South were apparent as early as 1787, at the Constitutional Convention in Philadelphia. Many northern delegates wanted to prohibit the importation of slaves. When southerners objected, the northerners settled for a provision that postponed the decision for twenty-one years. In return, the southerners agreed to let the federal government impose a tax on slaves who were imported into the country. Some northern delegates also objected to provisions in the Constitution that made slavery an acceptable institution. Southern delegates were equally dissatisfied with several measures that favored northern shipping interests over southern agricultural interests. In the end, both sides agreed to compromise, and slavery remained a part of American life.

These sectional disagreements reemerged as the country expanded westward. The majority of northerners acknowledged that the national economy of the mid-nineteenth century was largely dependent on southern agriculture, which in turn depended on slaves. Even so, many northerners did not want to see slavery extended into the new territories. Southerners insisted that, because the Constitution considered slaves property, they could bring these people with them, just as they would bring their furniture or livestock, if they decided to move west.

Frederick Douglass escaped to the North at a time when the slavery debate was growing more heated. With his talent as a speaker and his firsthand stories of slave life, he became a dynamic leader in the fight to achieve freedom and fairness for blacks. Douglass astounded the world with the power of his voice and his vivid writing, but his greatest asset was his courage. He was not afraid to champion unpopular causes or to speak up for his beliefs. The inner strength he had discovered as a teenage slave enabled him to persevere in his struggle for equality and to endure the frustrations and humiliations he would encounter along the way.

2. Growing Up in Slavery

Frederick Douglass was born on the Eastern Shore of Chesapeake Bay, about 12 miles (19 km) from Easton, Maryland. His birthday was in February 1818. He never knew the exact day. He did not know the identity of his father either, although he later heard that his father was probably his white master. His mother, Harriet Bailey, named him Frederick Augustus Washington Bailey. Harriet was a slave, which meant that her children were slaves as well. The family belonged to a man named Aaron Anthony.

Frederick was raised in a backwoods cabin by his grandmother, Betsy Bailey. Aaron Anthony allowed Betsy to live in her own cabin rather than in the slave quarters because she performed two useful services. Betsy was a midwife who delivered babies for the slaves on the plantation that Anthony managed. She also took care of her young grandchildren, so that Harriet could work in the fields.

Harriet Bailey died when Frederick was quite young, and, because she rarely had time to visit him,

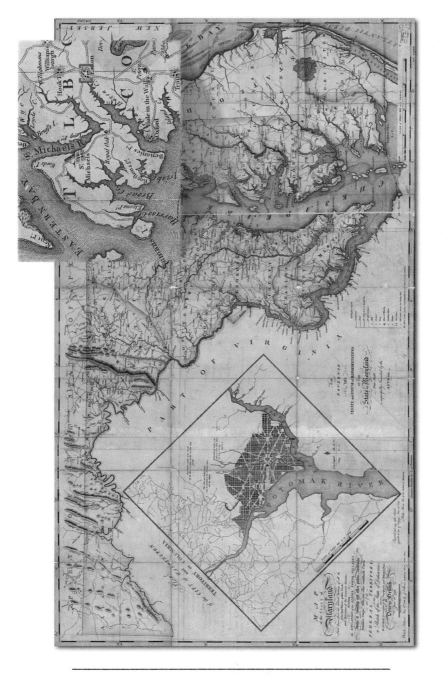

A map of the state of Maryland, engraved in 1794 by J. Thackara and J. Vallance, shows the rounded arm of the Eastern Shore to the east of Chesapeake Bay. The approximate location of Easton, Maryland, is indicated in red brackets (*inset*).

Frederick had few memories of his mother. His grandmother was the center of his life until he was old enough to be put to work on the plantation. Aaron Anthony ordered that the children in Betsy Bailey's care be brought to the main house when they reached a manageable age. One day, in 1824, when Frederick was about six years old, Betsy Bailey took him on the 12-mile (19-km) trek to Wye Plantation, where their master, Anthony, lived and worked as the estate's manager. The plantation was situated on the Wye River and was owned by a wealthy man named Colonel Edward Lloyd. Young Frederick followed his loving grandmother, ignorant of the turn his life was about to take.

When they arrived at the plantation, Betsy Bailey left Frederick in the slave quarters with some other slave children and quietly slipped away. The boy was heartbroken when he discovered that she was gone. Frederick's older brother and two sisters were already living at Wye, but they were almost strangers to young Frederick. He was alone in an unfamiliar world.

More than a dozen slaves worked in Wye House, a handsome white mansion with broad lawns, well-tended gardens, and elegant furnishings. Numerous other slaves tended the crops that grew on the plantation's 10,000 acres (4,047 ha). Colonel Lloyd had a reputation among his fellow planters for being good to the slaves who worked the plantation. In reality, Lloyd had very little to do with them. Anthony and a team of white overseers, including the cruel Austin Gore, were in charge of the slaves and punished the blacks whenever they pleased.

Frederick and the other black children were left in the care of Anthony's cook, a slave called Aunt Katy. She gave the children very little food and made them sleep wherever they could find a place. Frederick's bed was the floor of a storage closet. Fortunately Frederick found a friend in Anthony's daughter, Lucretia, who lived in her father's house with her husband, Thomas Auld. Lucretia became very fond of the little boy and would often give him food when Aunt Katy was not around.

Frederick was a bright and sociable child, which made him a good choice as the companion and errand boy to one of the Lloyd sons, Daniel. Brighter and more sociable slaves often became house servants. Other slaves worked in the fields or the stables. Daniel Lloyd was about five years older than Frederick, but the two quickly became

Of overseer Austin Gore, Frederick later wrote, " . . . under him there was more suffering from violence and bloodshed" than ever before. In an 1881 illustration, Gore is shown shooting Bill Denby, a slave who had refused to be whipped.

close friends. Frederick was soon spending quite a bit of time at Wye House, observing the way rich, white families lived. He was impressed with their fine furniture and beautiful clothes, but he was most fascinated by the way they talked. With a quick ear for imitation, Frederick soon abandoned his slave dialect, which was based on several African languages mixed with English, in favor of the formal English of an educated white gentleman.

The more Lucretia Auld saw of Frederick, the more she became convinced that he was too smart to grow up in the small world of rural Maryland. To give him a more stimulating life, she arranged to have him sent to Baltimore in March 1826. Frederick moved into the home of Lucretia's husband's brother, Hugh Auld, and his wife, Sophia, to help them take care of their two-year-old son, Tommy. Because Frederick was only eight years old himself, he probably did no more than keep the child entertained when Sophia was busy.

Frederick took to city life at once. He loved the busy streets, the rows of shops, and the bustling harbor with its ships carrying goods from all over the world. Above all, he loved Sophia Auld, who treated him as if he were her own child. For the first time in his life, Frederick slept in a real bed and ate his meals with his master's family. Sophia Auld often read to her son from the Bible, and Frederick was invited to join them. Fascinated by what he later called "the mystery of reading," he asked Sophia to teach him how to read. She was

W. J. Bennett's 1830s engraving shows Baltimore from the heights of Federal Hill. The harbor is filled with ships, and the bustling city center rises in the background. In the first decades of the nineteenth century, Baltimore grew to be the second-largest city in the United States.

so thrilled by his rapid progress that she showed her husband how well Frederick was doing. Instead of being impressed, Hugh Auld was angry. Teaching a slave to read was a dangerous practice, he told her. Once Frederick learned to read, Hugh argued, he would want to learn to write, and once he could write, he would run away. A slave should know nothing but the will of his master.

Hugh Auld's attitude was common among slave owners. Many books, including the Bible, discussed the inequities between slaves and their masters and championed the importance of personal freedom. An educated slave would not only be more inclined to run away but also find it easier to pass as a free man if he managed to escape. As Frederick later wrote, "To make a contented slave, you must make a thoughtless one. It is necessary to darken his moral and mental vision, and, as far as possible, to annihilate his power of reason."

Sophia abandoned Frederick's lessons, but he found a way to continue them on his own. Hugh owned a shipbuilding business not far from his house. Frederick often visited it. He noticed that the men marked the various lengths of lumber with letters that indicated where they were to be placed on a ship. The letter *S*, for instance, indicated that a board was to be placed on the starboard, or right-hand, side of the hull. The letters *S.A.* meant that it also went aft, or to the rear, of the ship.

Frederick saw the same letters in the spelling book that Tommy Auld brought home from school. By studying the letters in the book, Frederick taught himself to write the alphabet. When no one was around, he began copying some of Tommy's spelling words. Next he began picking up discarded newspapers on the street and trying to figure out what they said.

It was also at the shipyard that Frederick became friends with a group of white boys who would serve as his teachers. Frederick always carried a copy of Noah Webster's *American Spelling Book* with him, and he would pay the local white boys with pieces of bread to teach him to read the text.

Frederick and the Aulds were saddened when they received word that Frederick would have to return to Wye Plantation. Aaron Anthony had died nearly a year before, on November 14, 1826, and his possessions, including his slaves, were to be appraised and divided among his children. Lucretia inherited Frederick, who was only nine years old. According to Frederick's autobiography *The Life of Frederick Douglass*, Lucretia promptly sent him back to Baltimore and died the following month. Soon after, her brother Andrew died as well. Their property was divided among Lucretia's husband Thomas and several people unknown to Frederick. Frederick's grandmother, who had grown crippled in her service to the Anthonys, was sent to live in a small hut in the woods. She was cut off from her family and was forced to support herself. Frederick, who became the property of Thomas Auld after Lucretia's death, was more fortunate. He was allowed to stay with Hugh and Sophia Auld in Baltimore, until his owner forced him to move.

3. Hard Lessons

Frederick Bailey devoured knowledge in all of its forms. Sophia Auld's readings from the Bible further inspired Frederick's curiosity, especially in matters of religion. Around 1831, Frederick began to attend a Sunday school for free black children at Bethel African Methodist Episcopal Church. Two years later, Frederick started teaching at the school. Tommy Auld no longer needed a playmate, so Frederick was put to work in the shipyard as a messenger and general assistant. When he was not working, Frederick could usually be found with some of the other young slaves who worked along the waterfront. Their conversation was often of slavery.

One day Frederick heard the boys at the shipyard discussing a speech from *The Columbian Orator*, a collection of speeches by some of the world's most famous orators. Determined to own it, Frederick scraped together enough money to buy a copy. After reading the speeches of the great orators of the past, Frederick was captivated.

John Lewis Krimmel painted this watercolor of an African Methodist church service being held in a city alley. Krimmel's painting shows parishioners raising their arms and falling to the ground. Though exaggerated, this image illustrates the intensity and excitement that was common in black and white churches at the time.

Frederick's relatively pleasant life in Baltimore came to an abrupt end when he was about fifteen years old. His cousin Henny had been living with Thomas Auld and his second wife, Rowena, in St. Michael's, a small port on Chesapeake Bay. Rowena Auld regularly complained that Henny, who had been severely burned as a child, was too disabled to do any work. Rowena refused to care for Henny while her brother-in-law had possession of Frederick, an able-bodied slave who belonged to Thomas. Rowena prevailed upon her husband to send

Henny to Hugh and Sophia Auld. They agreed to take Henny, but, when she proved to be too much of a burden, they asked the Aulds for permission to send her back. Thomas said yes, but only if Frederick came with her. Frederick was sent away once again, to live with Thomas and Rowena in St. Michael's.

In his new home, Frederick Bailey found himself longing for the Sunday school classes he had taught in Baltimore. With the help of a man named Mr. Wilson, Frederick organized his own classes, inviting a dozen of St. Michael's slaves to attend. The first class was a great success, but the second time the group met, teachers from the white Methodist Sunday school and several white church members, including Thomas Auld, burst in on the class. Demanding to know if Frederick wanted to be hanged as was the famous rebel slave Nat Turner, the men threatened to beat the slaves if they did not stop the class at once.

Frederick bitterly resented Thomas Auld's role in the dissolution of the Sunday school. Frederick was also angry because Thomas, at his wife's insistence, used to beat Frederick's cousin Henny for not being more helpful around the house. To add to his resentments, Frederick often went hungry in Rowena's kitchen. Weighed down by these thoughts, Frederick became sullen and rebellious.

To crush his young slave's rebellious spirit, Thomas hired out Frederick to a man named Edward Covey,

Nat Turner, with arm outstretched, preaches to a gathering of slaves in the forest. Many southerners blamed the northern abolition movement for Turner's insurrection, refusing to believe that slaves could have conceived of and organized a large-scale rebellion.

Nat Turner was a Virginian slave with a deep interest in religion and a talent for preaching. In 1831, he enlisted about seventy other slaves in a rebellion that left nearly sixty whites dead, including Turner's master and his master's family. The rebellion was quickly crushed, and many of the slaves, including Turner, were hanged. The insurrection aroused fear in the white population and led to the enactment of stricter slave laws. Southern and northern states strengthened laws against educating blacks, both enslaved and free.

who owned a farm about 7 miles (11 km) from St. Michael's. Covey ran his farm with the labor of other men's slaves and paid the slaves' owners for their work. His strict rules and harsh discipline had earned him a reputation as a slave breaker. After a few months of hard work and regular beatings, even the most stubborn slaves became obedient.

Having spent most of his life in a city, Frederick Bailey had no experience with farm animals. When Covey ordered him to drive an oxcart into a nearby forest to gather wood, Frederick lost control of the oxen, which charged off without their driver. Covey immediately ordered the young man back into the woods, cut three switches from a large tree, and lashed him across the back. That brutal punishment was the first of many such beatings.

One scorching day in August, a group of slaves, including Frederick and another hired slave named Bill Smith, were at work husking wheat. Each man depended on the other to do the work as a team. Halfway through the job, Frederick collapsed with sunstroke. Moments later, Covey appeared and demanded to know why Bill had stopped working. Bill explained that Frederick was sick and that, without Frederick, Bill could not do his part of the job.

Covey approached Frederick, gave him a kick, and ordered him to get up. Frederick tried to obey, but he was too weak to stand. Covey kicked him again and

At Edward Covey's farm, Frederick Bailey worked in the fields and tended the animals. In this pencil sketch by Edwin Forbes, made on September 26, 1863, slaves on a farm near Culpeper Court House, Virginia, are at work stacking wheat.

struck him on the head with a wooden board. With blood running from his head, Frederick stumbled into the woods. Covey called to him to come back. Frederick ignored him, but Covey, aware that the slave would have to return sooner or later, let him go. Frederick made his way back to St. Michael's, told Thomas Auld what had happened, and begged his master not to send him back. Auld refused. Frederick could stay for the night but he was to return to Covey's farm the next day.

Knowing that he could expect another whipping, Frederick did not go back right away. He left St. Michael's on a Saturday morning, hid out in the woods for a day, and spent Saturday night in the cabin of a free black man who worked on some of the local farms. When Frederick arrived at Covey's, it was Sunday morning. Instead of beating Frederick, Covey smiled and drove off to church.

Believing himself to be a God-fearing man, Covey did not beat his slaves on Sunday. By Monday, however, things changed. At dawn, Covey found Frederick at work in the barn, climbing a ladder to the stable loft. Covey grabbed Frederick by the leg to drag him onto the stable floor and tried to tie his legs with a rope, but Frederick was too quick for him. He jumped down and landed on top of Covey. The two men wrestled for a few minutes, and then Frederick grabbed Covey by the throat. When Covey called for help, his cousin appeared and tried to drag Frederick away. The slave gave Covey's cousin a kick that sent him staggering away. The fight did not end until Frederick relaxed his grip and told Covey there would be trouble if the slave breaker ever beat Frederick again.

Frederick completed his year at Edward Covey's without any further beatings and returned to St. Michael's for Christmas. At the beginning of 1835, Thomas Auld hired Frederick out to another farmer, William Freeland. Frederick later called Freeland "the best master I ever had, till I became my own master."

Frederick made a number of friends at Freeland's farm, including brothers John and Henry Harris. As Frederick grew closer to the Harris brothers, he felt free to tell them about his hopes of running away. They all agreed that William Freeland was a good master, but they also agreed that they hated being slaves. Before long, the three men joined forces with three other slaves and began hatching a plot to escape.

Frederick had spent enough time on the Baltimore waterfront to know that it would be a short journey north on Chesapeake Bay to the Susquehanna River. About 20 miles (32 km) upriver from Chesapeake Bay, the Susquehanna River crosses the border between Maryland and Pennsylvania. If the slaves could get their hands on a large canoe, they could paddle to the head of Chesapeake Bay in the dark of night. When they got to the Susquehanna River, they would leave the canoe and walk the rest of the way to the free state of Pennsylvania. As did many fugitive slaves, they would use the North Star as their guide.

The week before they were to leave, Frederick forged and signed notes for each of his partners. The notes said, "This is to certify, that I, the undersigned, have given the bearer, my servant, full liberty to go to Baltimore, to spend the Easter holidays. Written with my own hand, &c."

One slave backed out at the last minute. The others were still determined to escape. On the morning of the appointed day, as Frederick started toward the Freeland house for breakfast, he saw four white men on horses leading two of his friends with their hands tied behind their backs. The four men were neighbors of William Freeland. Frederick did not know how they had heard of the planned escape, but he suspected that the slave who had backed out might have told them. When Frederick reached the kitchen, one of the white men seized him and another tied his hands. They attempted to do the same to the Harris brothers when they arrived, but Henry resisted. There was a scuffle, and, in the confusion, Frederick managed to toss his counterfeit note into the fire.

$150 REWARD

RANAWAY from the subscriber, on the night of the 2d instant, a negro man, who calls himself *Henry May*, about 22 years old, 5 feet 6 or 8 inches high, ordinary color, rather chunky built, bushy head, and has it divided mostly on one side, and keeps it very nicely combed; has been raised in the house, and is a first rate dining-room servant, and was in a tavern in Louisville for 18 months. I expect he is now in Louisville trying to make his escape to a free state, (in all probability to Cincinnati, Ohio.) Perhaps he may try to get employment on a steamboat. He is a good cook, and is handy in any capacity as a house servant. Had on when he left, a dark cassinett coatee, and dark striped cassinett pantaloons, new—he had other clothing. I will give $50 reward if taken in Louisvill; 100 dollars if taken one hundred miles from Louisville in this State, and 150 dollars if taken out of this State, and delivered to me, or secured in any jail so that I can get him again.
WILLIAM BURKE.
Bardstown, Ky., September 3d, 1838.

Slave owners would go to great lengths to find their runaway slaves. In 1838, this advertisement appeared in a local newspaper on behalf of slave owner William Burke of Bardstown, Kentucky. It includes a physical description of a twenty-two-year-old runaway slave named Henry May and offers upward of $150, or about $2,400 today, for his return.

The white men, with the would-be runaways leashed to their saddles, began the journey from Freeland's farm, which was on the outskirts of St. Michael's, to the jail in the town of Easton. On the way, Frederick told the others to destroy their passes, and they all agreed not to reveal their plan. Frederick, who was the best-educated member of the group, was assumed to be the ringleader of the plot. For this reason, the culprits were first taken to Thomas Auld's store in St. Michael's, where the slave catchers presented Frederick to his master. The slave catchers demanded that all five blacks be hanged immediately. Auld was suspicious of Frederick and the other slaves, but he resisted the idea of having them hanged.

Thomas Auld may have been genuinely concerned about Frederick, or he may only have been trying to protect his property. In any case, he succeeded in calming down the slave catchers. The slaves were led away in ropes to the town jail in Easton, where their fates would be decided.

The captives waited and worried behind bars while a town official reviewed the case. With no sign of the counterfeit passes, there was no evidence that the slaves had been planning to escape and nothing to do but send them back to their owners. The other slaves were released to their masters, but Auld did not appear to claim Frederick. It occurred to Frederick that Auld might be planning to sell him to a southern slave trader.

If so, his hopes of escaping to the North would be gone. Few slaves escaped from the Deep South. The North was simply too far away.

Frederick stayed in jail for a full week while his master thought about what to do with the rebellious slave. Frederick was capable and clever, his master had surely noticed, but living in St. Michael's had turned him into a troublemaker. When Auld finally came to retrieve his young slave, he told Frederick that he was sending him, in the care of a friend, to Alabama. In Alabama, Frederick would work for eight years and then be set free. When the friend failed to appear, Auld decided to send Frederick back to Hugh Auld in Baltimore. If Frederick learned a trade and became a skilled laborer, he could be hired out and the Aulds would get his wages. Thomas Auld also promised Frederick that if he worked hard and behaved himself, Auld would free Frederick on his twenty-fifth birthday.

4. A Great Escape

Frederick was dubious about Thomas Auld's promise. Even if Auld kept his word, Frederick's twenty-fifth birthday was seven or eight years away. Still Frederick was eager to return to Baltimore. He enjoyed more freedom in the city than he could ever find on the Eastern Shore.

Hugh Auld arranged for Frederick to become an apprentice in one of Baltimore's shipyards. Frederick worked with an experienced caulker, or a person who applies tar to the seams of ships to make them watertight. The white apprentices, fearing any black men who might take away their jobs, instantly disliked Frederick. On several occasions, they taunted him and tried to start fights. Frederick, who was taller and stronger than most young men his age, easily fought off the troublemakers. Eventually four of the white apprentices joined forces, and Frederick was outnumbered. They pummeled him with their fists, one of them hit him with a brick, and another whacked him with a heavy metal bar. One man kicked the fallen Frederick in the face, and the slave's eye bled and swelled.

In the early nineteenth century, eastern cities were built around busy shipyards and docks. In Baltimore, Frederick Bailey began his apprenticeship in William Gardiner's shipyard, which would have looked much like the Smith and Dimon Shipyard in Manhattan, shown here in an 1833 illustration by James Pringle.

Douglass later wrote, "I am almost amazed that I was not murdered outright, in that ship yard, so murderous was the spirit which prevailed there."

When Frederick returned home battered and bleeding, Hugh Auld was furious. He demanded that the attackers be arrested for assaulting his property. However, none of the white workmen who had witnessed the assault were willing to testify on behalf of a slave, and Frederick's testimony could not be admitted in court because he was black. Auld's request was denied.

Hugh Auld found a new place for Frederick at a ship-yard where there were several other black caulkers. Frederick was a good worker, and before long he was earning up to nine dollars per week. However, Frederick was obligated to give every penny to Hugh Auld.

The next time Thomas Auld came to Baltimore on business, Frederick proposed a different arrangement. Frederick would find his own work as a caulker and keep a portion of his wages. In return, he would move out of the Aulds' house and pay to live somewhere else. This was a common practice in Baltimore. It appealed to slave owners, because they could continue to earn money from the labor of slaves without the expense of housing and feeding them.

To Frederick's disappointment, Thomas Auld rejected the idea. He was afraid it would give Frederick too many opportunities to get into trouble. Frederick let the matter drop, but, two months later, he presented his plan to Hugh Auld. Hugh, seeing some merit in the arrangement, agreed to let Frederick move out of the Aulds' house with the promise that he would return faithfully every Saturday evening and give Auld three dollars of his pay.

Frederick was sure that, under this new arrangement, he could save enough money to escape. Meanwhile, he was no longer subject to the rules of Hugh Auld's house-hold. He was free to come and go as he pleased, giving him the opportunity to socialize with some of Baltimore's free blacks, including a housekeeper named Anna

Murray who also came from the Eastern Shore. She and Frederick were soon talking about marriage.

Frederick Bailey may have thought seriously of remaining in Baltimore and becoming part of its black community. If so, he changed his mind after the events that began one Saturday evening. He was delayed at work and in a hurry to go to a church meeting some miles (km) outside of the city. Instead of delivering his three dollars to Hugh Auld on schedule, Frederick waited until the following Monday. Auld rebuked Frederick for failing to show up on Saturday and forced him to give up his private lodgings. It was a crushing blow to Frederick. If he and Anna married, they would not be able to live together and would see each other only on their days off. Frederick decided it was time to escape.

Anna Murray, shown here in an undated photograph, spent her life savings helping Frederick Bailey escape from slavery, and she devoted the rest of her life to taking care of his household and their children.

To avoid arousing Auld's suspicions, Frederick became a model slave. He worked hard and at the end of every week handed over his wages without a word of complaint. Auld was so pleased that he rewarded Frederick with a gift of twenty-five cents and urged him to make good use of it. Frederick assured Auld that he would.

Frederick started planning his escape in the summer of 1838. Rumor had it that the locations of some of the safe houses along the Underground Railroad had been discovered and that the authorities were keeping a close watch on them. After some consideration, Frederick boldly chose to escape by train. His traveling clothes would be similar to those worn by the crewmen of ships docked in Baltimore's harbor. A sailor's outfit was the perfect disguise. He had the rugged build of a seaman, and he was familiar with the language of ships. Furthermore, free black men often found work on ships.

The law required free blacks to carry papers when they traveled so that they would not be arrested as slaves. Anna Murray had given Frederick enough money to pay his train fare, but he could not afford to buy forged papers. He borrowed a set of seaman's papers from a free, retired black sailor. The papers had the other man's name and description on them, but they looked suitably official. Frederick would travel alone and send for Anna when he had safely arrived in the North.

On September 3, 1838, Frederick climbed aboard the train headed north. He planned to make New York the first stop on his flight to freedom. After that, he was not sure where he would settle. Frederick was relieved to

Between 1820 and 1855, community leader and abolitionist William Jackson lived in this house in Newton, Massachusetts. The house was a station on the Underground Railroad. Runaway slaves would hide in the basement or cellar and eat a simple meal before moving on to the next station and, hopefully, to freedom in Canada.

The Underground Railroad was an informal network of safe houses set up by black and white abolitionists to help fugitive slaves. The abolitionists gave the refugees, who were mostly young, healthy males, food and shelter and directed them to the next stop on the route. The end of the line was Canada, where American fugitive slave laws could not be enforced. Many blacks stopped before they got that far, settling in one of the free states and changing their names to avoid capture. However, most runaways, confronted with the challenges of escape, returned to their masters in only a few days.

find that the rail-
road car set aside for
black passengers was
crowded. At the train
conductor's request,
Frederick presented
his seaman's papers.
The conductor al-
ready had his hands
full collecting tick-
ets. He barely glanced
at Frederick's sea-
man's papers before
punching the slave's
ticket and going on
his way.

If a sailor was captured or forced into service by the enemy, he would have to prove that he was a U.S. citizen. Twenty-year-old free black sailor Samuel Fox carried this certificate, issued by the government, as proof of his American citizenship. Frederick Bailey carried a similar document during his escape to the North.

Afraid to visit one of New York City's black board-inghouses, which were often watched by slave catchers, Frederick spent his first nights of freedom sleeping on the wharves in the harbor. Soon a friendly sailor intro-duced the fugitive slave, who called himself Frederick Johnson, to a man named David Ruggles, the secre-tary of an organization that helped runaway slaves. Ruggles offered Frederick a place to stay and money to continue his journey, and Frederick accepted. He waited several days for Anna to arrive, and the couple married soon after.

5. A New Last Name

David Ruggles advised Frederick and Anna Johnson to settle in New Bedford, Massachusetts. The city was not only a prosperous whaling port, but also it had a large shipbuilding industry where Frederick could find work. In addition, New Bedford was one of the strongholds of the abolitionist movement. The city had a large population of Quakers, who were among the leaders in the fight to abolish slavery.

The abolition of slavery was not a new idea. The first American antislavery organization, the Society for the Relief of Free Negroes Unlawfully Held in Bondage, was organized in 1775. Within a few years, concerned citizens in New York, Delaware, Maryland, Rhode Island, and Connecticut organized similar groups.

Around 1820, a new and more militant abolitionist movement got underway. It started as a one-man crusade by a Quaker newspaper publisher named Benjamin Lundy. He was soon joined by a fiery New Englander named William Lloyd Garrison. The two men began writing and preaching about the evils of slavery,

Southerners called for the capture, the imprisonment, and even the execution of abolitionist William Lloyd Garrison, shown here in an oil portrait by Nathaniel Jocelyn made in 1833. Of the fight against slavery Garrison wrote, "I am in earnest—I will not equivocate—I will not excuse—I will not retreat a single inch—and *I will be heard.*"

insisting that it be abolished. Antislavery organizations were revived in several states, and, in 1833, they banded together to form the American Anti-Slavery Society. The Massachusetts Anti-Slavery Society was a particularly active branch of the national organization, and many of its members lived in New Bedford.

David Ruggles had given Frederick and Anna Johnson the address of a black couple, Mary and Nathan Johnson, who would help them to get settled in the whaling port. The Johnsons were pleased to meet the new arrivals, but were perhaps annoyed to discover that they had the same last name. According to Nathan, "Johnson" was a common last name among New Bedford blacks, and he suggested that Frederick consider something else. Nathan, who was reading Sir Walter Scott's poem "The Lady of the Lake," recommended the last name of one of the characters in the poem, James Douglas. Failing to notice that Scott's character had only one "s" in his name, Frederick spelled it with a second "s."

The people of Massachusetts turned out to be much less tolerant than Frederick Douglass had been led to believe. When he applied for work as a caulker in New Bedford's shipyards, he was told that they never hired blacks because the white caulkers would not work with them. His only choice was to become a day laborer, picking up odd jobs such as digging cellars, collecting trash, or shoveling coal. The pay was barely enough on which to live. The Douglasses rented a small house, and, within the next few years, Anna gave birth to a daughter and a son.

At the New Bedford Zion Methodist Church, Douglass became one of the congregation's most faithful members, serving as a Sunday school teacher and lay preacher. His only complaint about the church was that its pastors never mentioned slavery in their sermons. When he asked them why, they told him it was too controversial.

Douglass disagreed. He had strong opinions on the subject, and he wanted to make them known. He got his chance when a church meeting was called to discuss the colonization movement, which was working to send blacks back to Africa. Most of the people

Many well-meaning Americans saw colonization as the answer to slavery. In 1817, the newly organized American Colonization Society bought land on the west coast of Africa and created the country of Liberia. The society raised thousands of dollars to purchase slaves and send them to the new nation and to transport free blacks who wanted to join them. By 1860, more than 11,000 blacks had made the journey. Since then, Liberia has suffered from a huge national debt, attempted European colonization, and civil war. The majority of the country's current citizens are members of various African tribes. About 2.5 percent are the descendants of former American slaves.

at the church meeting were against it, and they voiced their objections in mild tones. Frederick Douglass was more outspoken. He denounced the idea of shipping slaves back to Africa. The vast majority of slave families had been in America for one hundred years or more. They were Americans, and they would be better served by being given their freedom at home, in America.

Frederick Douglass had another chance to speak when the Zion Church appointed a new pastor, a former slave from upstate New York named Thomas James. James never hesitated to condemn slavery, not only from the pulpit but also at the numerous antislavery meetings that were held in New Bedford.

On one such occasion, the pastor spotted Douglass in the audience and asked him to speak about his experiences as a slave. Douglass spoke so persuasively that he was invited to talk at other meetings. At one such meeting, abolitionist William C. Coffin invited Douglass to speak at the upcoming meeting of the Massachusetts Anti-Slavery Society, an event that would catapult Douglass into the spotlight.

The meeting was held on the island of Nantucket, Massachusetts, in August 1841. Several hundred people were present, including the country's best-known abolitionist, William Lloyd Garrison. When Douglass got to his feet to speak, he was nervous and became confused. He spoke haltingly at first. After a few minutes, he found his voice and the words came pouring out. He told his own story, the tale of a runaway slave, and he told it so well that his white audience was spellbound. When he finished, there were cheers and shouts of approval. William Lloyd Garrison rushed to shake his hand, and John A. Collins of the Massachusetts Anti-Slavery Society asked Douglass to become one of their regular speakers. The society would pay him a salary and would help him to buy a house in Lynn, near the society's headquarters in Boston.

With his rich voice and imposing presence, Douglass was a unique force on the speaker's platform. His eye-witness accounts of the mistreatment of slaves breathed life into the abolitionists' arguments. People who were indifferent to the problem often changed their minds after hearing him speak. He could make his listeners laugh by poking fun at the slaveholders he had met. In the next breath, he would have the audience in tears as he described the treatment of slaves.

Soon Douglass was asked to become a speaker for the American Anti-Slavery Society. His new role took him beyond the boundaries of Massachusetts and made him a national figure. None of the other speakers he appeared with, including William Lloyd Garrison, could match his burning eloquence. There are few records of Douglass's early speeches, but later transcriptions show the force of his oratory. In a speech in 1850, Douglass said, "Go where you may, search where you will, roam through all the monarchies and despotisms of the old world, travel through South America, search out every abuse, and when you have found the last, lay your facts by the side of the every-day practices of this nation, and you will say with me, that, for revolting barbarity and shameless hypocrisy, America reigns without a rival."

Fellow abolitionist and suffragist Elizabeth Cady Stanton once described Douglass as "an African prince, majestic in his wrath." Stanton's comment reflects the white abolitionists' constant awareness of Douglass's race. Although abolitionists were sincerely concerned about blacks, many white abolitionists never accepted them as equals. To all but a few of his associates in the movement, Douglass was an admired coworker who was useful to their cause, but never a personal friend.

Though overshadowed by her colleague Susan B. Anthony, Elizabeth Cady Stanton was a powerful player in the women's rights movement from its beginning. This photograph of Stanton dates from the mid- to late-nineteenth century.

Douglass was not surprised by the abolitionists' attitudes. In his travels around the country, he had come to see that racial prejudice was as prevalent in the North as it was in the South. At a stop in Indiana, he was attacked by a mob shouting insults and throwing rotten eggs. One of the rioters struck Douglass, breaking Douglass's right hand. The break was not properly set, and Douglass never recovered the full use of his hand.

Less dangerous but no less frustrating were the laws that required blacks to be segregated from whites in public places. More than once, Douglass boarded a train with a first-class ticket and was ordered to sit in the "Jim Crow car." On one occasion, he refused, and the conductor enlisted the help of several colleagues to drag Douglass out. On another trip Frederick Douglass demanded to know why he could not sit in first class. The train conductor told him bluntly, "Because you are black."

Douglass liked to relate these stories in his speeches to

This engraving, entitled *Negro Expulsion from Railway Car, Philadelphia*, appeared in the *Illustrated London News* of September 27, 1856. A black passenger is angrily asked to leave a car occupied by white travelers.

remind his abolitionist friends that, despite their support for blacks, they and fellow northerners were capable of racism. "Prejudice against color is stronger north than south," Douglass maintained. "I have met it at every step the three years I have been out of southern slavery. . . ."

As Douglass traveled around the country, his speaking style matured and changed. After causing a sensation with his shocking stories about slavery in his early speeches for the Massachusetts Anti-Slavery Society and the American Anti-Slavery Society, Douglass decided to take a more thoughtful approach. He began talking about the history of the institution and its unfortunate moral consequences. His colleagues in the antislavery movement begged him to stop. He did not fit the image of a simple slave, and people were already whispering that he was an impostor. If he spoke as an educated man, they would consider their suspicions confirmed.

Stunned that anyone would suggest that he was not who and what he claimed to be, Frederick Douglass resolved to write his autobiography. When it was published, there would be no further doubt that he was telling the truth.

6. The *North Star*

In 1845, the Anti-Slavery office in Boston published Frederick Douglass's first book, the *Narrative of the Life of Frederick Douglass, an American Slave*. In it, Douglass describes his early life in Maryland, his fight with Edward Covey, his experiences in Baltimore, and the story of his escape to the North. The narrative contained enough detail to convince his critics that he was not an impostor. The book was an instant success. Within a few months, 4,500 copies had been sold, and three editions had been published in Europe. Within five years, the sales had risen to 30,000.

With Douglass rapidly becoming an international celebrity, the leaders of the American Anti-Slavery Society decided to send him on a fund-raising trip to Great Britain. Great Britain had abolished slavery a few years earlier, and the British abolitionist movement

Next page: In his preface to the first edition of Frederick Douglass's *Narrative of the Life of Frederick Douglass, an American Slave*, William Lloyd Garrison wrote of Douglass, "There is in him that union of head and heart, which is indispensable to an enlightenment of the heads and a winning of the hearts of others."

NARRATIVE

OF THE

LIFE

OF

FREDERICK DOUGLASS,

AN

AMERICAN SLAVE.

WRITTEN BY HIMSELF.

BOSTON:
PUBLISHED AT THE ANTI-SLAVERY OFFICE,
No. 25 CORNHILL.
1849

hoped to achieve similar success in other parts of the world. The trip had another, even more important, purpose. Douglass's book mentioned real names, dates, and places. Although the book had been published under his new name, anyone who had known him in Maryland would have no trouble recognizing the author as Frederick Bailey. As a fugitive slave, he could be arrested and returned to Thomas Auld. Douglass hoped to remain in Great Britain until the publicity from the book died down and it was safe to return to the United States.

Anna Douglass did not go abroad with her husband. Shy, illiterate, and ill at ease in public, she preferred to stay at home in Lynn, where she had plenty to keep her busy. By now the Douglasses had four young children: a daughter, Rosetta; and three sons; Lewis Henry, Frederick Jr., and Charles Remond.

Douglass's trip got off to a bad start. The ship's captain refused to give Douglass the first-class cabin he had paid for, so he had to travel in steerage, the cheapest and least comfortable accommodations. When he arrived in Great Britain, however, Douglass found no sign of racial prejudice. He drew enthusiastic crowds in England, Ireland, and Scotland. Many of his listeners made generous contributions to the antislavery cause.

After more than a year of traveling, Douglass was anxious to be reunited with his family, but he hesitated to go home. The authorities might be waiting to catch the fugitive slave the instant he set foot in the United

States. Douglass mentioned his worries to Ellen Richardson, a Quaker who was active in the British antislavery movement. As Douglass came to the end of his speaking tour, Richardson not only raised the money to buy his freedom, she enlisted her lawyer brother-in-law to handle the arrangements.

It was not unusual for slaveholders to grant slaves their freedom in return for a hefty price. Douglass learned, however, that earlier that year, Thomas Auld had sold Douglass to Hugh Auld and that Hugh had declared his intention of seizing the fugitive slave if he ever returned to the United States. After some negotiation, however, Hugh agreed to sell Douglass for $711.66, the equivalent of nearly $13,000 today. Hugh signed the necessary papers, received the payment, and Frederick Douglass became a legally free man.

Douglass returned to America on the same steamship that had brought him to Great Britain. Again he purchased a first-class ticket, and again he was given a lesser berth. Douglass described this treatment in a letter to the London *Times*. When newspapers throughout Great Britain took up Douglass's cause, an embarrassed Samuel Cunard, the owner of the British steamship line, issued a public apology.

During his trip abroad, Douglass had made plans to establish a newspaper for blacks on his return to the United States. His British friends had given him

This bill of sale, granting Frederick Douglass his freedom for a price of $711.66, bears Hugh Auld's signature. Some of his colleagues criticized Douglass for buying his freedom. They argued that in buying his freedom, Douglass accepted his status as property. In his 1855 biography, Douglass explained his actions by saying that he viewed the bill of sale "simply in the light of a ransom, or as money extorted by a robber."

the funds to get started, and he had already selected a name, the *North Star*. When he informed his associates at the American Anti-Slavery Society of his new venture, they tried to talk him out of it. The newspaper was a bad idea, they told him. His talents lay in speaking, not in writing. Besides, he would have a hard time selling such a paper. Douglass suspected that their real concern was that the *North Star* would attract black subscribers away from William Lloyd Garrison's abolitionist newspaper, the *Liberator*.

Hoping to persuade Douglass to abandon the *North Star*, the American Anti-Slavery Society hired him to

Amy Post and her husband, Isaac, were prominent social activists. They were forced to break from the Society of Friends, or Quakers, when the couple's political activism came into conflict with the religion's policy of noninvolvement.

write for their own publication, the *National Anti-Slavery Standard*. He published several articles and continued to tour the country making speeches. The society's directors assumed Douglass had lost interest in starting his own paper. A few months later, they were dismayed to discover that they were wrong.

In the fall of 1847, Douglass wrote to another member of the abolitionist movement, Amy Post, in Rochester, New York, to tell her that he had decided to establish the headquarters of the *North Star* in that upstate city. Amy and her husband, Isaac, were great admirers of Douglass, and he knew that they would help him in whatever way they could. Douglass was eager to leave Massachusetts and establish himself as separate from William Lloyd Garrison and the directors of the American Anti-Slavery Society.

Gerrit Smith was one of the first people to welcome Douglass to New York State. Smith had inherited a huge fortune, which he used to support such causes as temperance, prison reform, women's suffrage, and abolition. He also was one of the organizers of the anti-slavery Liberty Party. Unfortunately, the party was unable to attract many members and had little influence. In his letter of welcome to Douglass, Smith included a check to cover a subscription to the *North Star* and promised Douglass 40 acres (16 ha) of land in upper New York State. It was the first of many generous gifts that Frederick Douglass would receive from Gerrit Smith.

Gerrit Smith, shown here in an oil painting from the 1860s, was a champion of abolition and social equality. He housed runaway slaves, paid the legal fees of those accused of aiding runaways, and gave small farms in upstate New York to poor and homeless families.

The first issue of the *North Star* appeared on December 3, 1847. Despite his discovery that the costs of printing and mailing the periodical left him very little profit, Douglass was convinced he could make a success

Printed under the masthead of Douglass's *North Star* is the motto, "Right is of no Sex—Truth is of no Color—God is the Father of us all, and we are all Brethren." As this motto suggests, Douglass's paper campaigned not only for the abolition of slavery but also for the extension to women of all civil liberties, such as the right to vote.

of the weekly. He returned to Lynn to help Anna and the children get ready for the move to Rochester. With his family settled, Douglass returned to the antislavery lecture circuit and even mortgaged his house to supplement his income and support his struggling newspaper.

In the summer of 1848, he attended the country's first women's rights convention in Seneca Falls, New York. The event was organized by Elizabeth Cady Stanton and Lucretia Mott. In 1840, these two women had been barred from the floor of the World's Anti-Slavery Convention, held in London, England, because they were women. Since then, they had been determined to stage their own civil rights convention. In 1848, when Stanton stood up in the Methodist chapel in which the Seneca Falls convention was held and read a resolution declaring that women

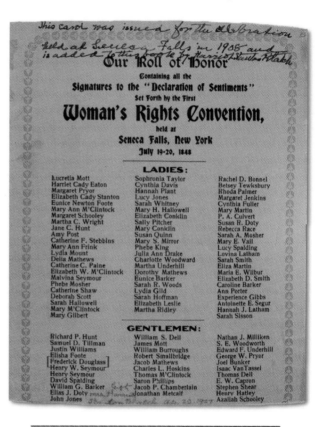

The "Roll of Honor" from the 1848 Women's Rights Convention lists Frederick Douglass's name, in red brackets, among the signers of the Declaration of Sentiments, Elizabeth Cady Stanton's statement of the rights of women.

should have the right to vote, even Mott was shocked. The only man in the audience who spoke out in support of Stanton was Frederick Douglass. Thanks to his eloquent speech in favor of women's suffrage, the resolution carried by a slim majority, and the women's rights group began their campaign for the right to vote.

Elizabeth Cady Stanton's enthusiasm inspired Douglass to start thinking about the power of the ballot box. Throughout his years as an abolitionist, Douglass had accepted William Lloyd Garrison's belief that slavery was an immoral institution that would be outlawed when enough people became convinced of its sinfulness. Garrison thought politics was an ignoble way to achieve a noble goal, and he had no use for the Constitution, because he believed it acknowledged slavery's right to exist. After attending the Seneca Falls meeting, Douglass came to suspect that Garrison's attitudes toward political reform and the U.S. Constitution were misguided.

7. Signs of Trouble

On March 22, 1849, Anna and Frederick Douglass welcomed another child into their family, a daughter named Annie. Two months after her arrival, they also acquired a houseguest, a white Englishwoman named Julia Griffiths. Griffiths had come to the United States to join the American abolitionist movement and to help Frederick Douglass run the *North Star*. She shocked even the supposedly tolerant abolitionists by moving in with the Douglasses. Whites and blacks rarely socialized, and it was particularly scandalous for a black man to become friends with a white woman. The abolitionists feared that Douglass's friendship with Julia Griffiths would drive supporters away from their cause. However, Griffiths's arrival proved to be a blessing for the *North Star*.

Douglass's speaking trips left him little time to tend to the details of the paper, and it was in serious financial trouble. A born businesswoman, Griffiths set to work. She soon reduced the publication's debt by $700. Griffiths was also a skilled editor and writer. Frederick Douglass was a master of the spoken word

Douglass, seated to the left of the woman in the white bonnet, appeared at countless conventions and assemblies to speak out against slavery and in favor of women's rights. This daguerreotype was taken at a convention held in Cazenovia, New York, in 1850.

but less sure of himself as a writer. Griffiths advised him on grammar, edited his articles, and read to him from great works of literature to familiarize him with the power and beauty of the written word.

The presence of Julia Griffiths in the Douglass household was the cause of at least one disagreement between Douglass and William Lloyd Garrison. Griffiths's presence might have played a part in creating the ever-widening gulf between the two men. The split between Douglass and Garrison, however, was also a matter of interpretation and principle. In essays and speeches, William Lloyd Garrison and like-minded abolitionists called for an immediate end to the institution of slavery. People who took a more realistic view of the situation knew that this was a vain hope. Slaveholders were as determined to hold on to their slaves as abolitionists were to set them free. Practical politicians looked for other solutions to the problem.

In 1818, the Missouri Territory had petitioned Congress to become a state. The territory had been settled largely by southerners, so politicians and citizens had assumed it would be a slave state. One northern congressman, James Tallmadge of New York, had fought the spread of slavery to the western frontier by presenting an amendment to the statehood bill that said no more slaves would be allowed into Missouri, and that slaves already living there would be freed at the age of twenty-five.

The proslavery members of Congress had rejected the amendment, and a debate had ensued. It had eventually been settled by the Missouri Compromise, which held that slavery could continue in Missouri but would be forbidden in future western territories north of the 36°30' north latitude. Missouri's admission to the Union would have given the slave states a majority in the Senate, however, thus allowing them to defeat antislavery legislation. Free-state politicians had granted statehood to Missouri only after Maine had applied for and had been granted admission as a free state, bringing the number of proslavery and antislavery senators back into balance.

Next spread: In the mid-nineteenth century, the West was carved into territories and states, sparking debate between free-soil and proslavery factions, both of which wanted to seize control of Congress. This map of the United States was published in 1849, by J. H. Colton.

With the annexation of Texas in 1845 and the acquisition of California, New Mexico, and Utah at the end of the Mexican War in 1848, Congress had been confronted with the same thorny problems. The arguments over the expansion of slavery became so ferocious that the South threatened to secede, or withdraw, from the Union. The crisis was avoided by the Compromise of 1850. Under the terms of the new law, California joined the Union as a free state, and the New Mexico–Texas border was established. To prevent any further arguments in Congress, the question of slavery in New Mexico and Utah was to be decided by the people who lived there, a solution known as popular sovereignty.

In return for southern support of the Compromise of 1850, Congress agreed to tighten the Fugitive Slave Law, which was originally enacted in 1793, but had never been very effective. The revised law provided for the appointment of special commissioners to seize and return runaway slaves and imposed severe penalties on anyone who interfered with the arrest of a fugitive or aided in his or her escape. In addition, the testimony of runaway slaves was not permitted in legal hearings, and fugitive slaves were not allowed jury trials. Abolitionists detested the new Fugitive Slave Law. They staged demonstrations, scheduled meetings, published pamphlets and newspaper articles, and defied the law by continuing to help runaway slaves.

Frederick Douglass did his share of speaking and writing against the law, but he had come to agree with Gerrit Smith. Preaching alone would never work. Political action within the framework of the law was the only way to change the system. In adopting Smith's beliefs, Douglass made a decisive break from William Lloyd Garrison, who continued to disdain politics. Garrison forbade the members of the American Anti-Slavery Society to have anything to do with a government that was founded on a proslavery document, the U.S. Constitution.

In 1851, Douglass publicly defied Garrison by praising the Constitution in the *North Star* and urging that it "be wielded in behalf of emancipation." To assert his independence further, he changed the name of the *North Star* to *Frederick Douglass' Paper*. Within the next few years, his friendship with Garrison came to a bitter end, and, in 1854, Douglass would stop attending meetings of the American Anti-Slavery Society.

In 1852, Frederick and Anna Douglass moved out of their Rochester home to a farmhouse about 2 miles (3 km) south of the city. The isolated house became an important stop on the Underground Railroad. Arriving under the cover of darkness, fugitive slaves could be safely hidden in the barn. Early the next morning, Amy and Isaac Post would escort them to the mouth of the Genesee River and to a boat that would take them across Lake Ontario to Canada.

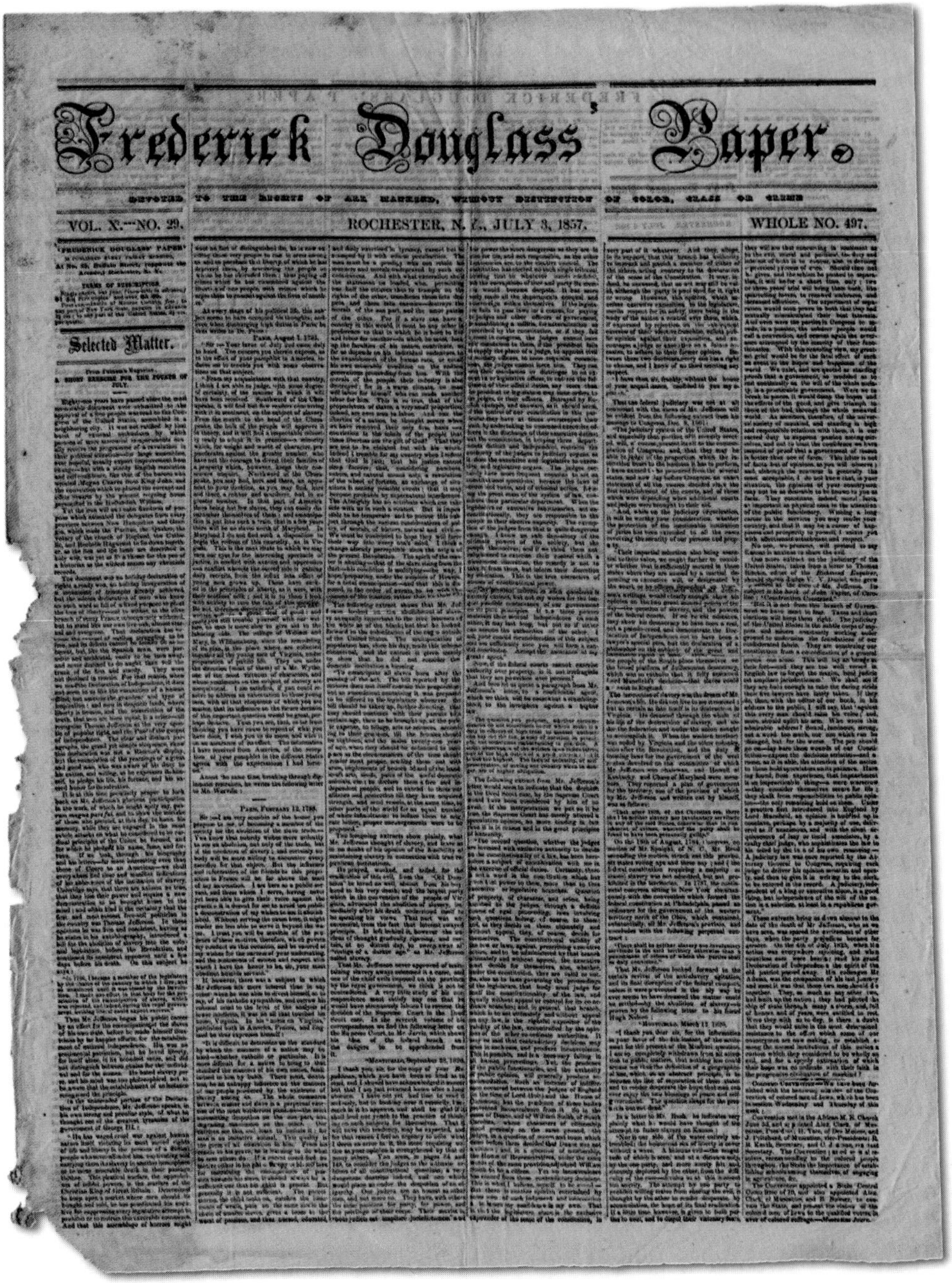

Frederick Douglass Paper.

VOL. X.—NO. 29.   ROCHESTER, N.Y., JULY 3, 1857.   WHOLE NO. 497.

Selected Matter.

In April 1851, Gerrit Smith offered to merge his unsuccessful *Liberty Party Paper* with Douglass's debt-ridden *North Star*. Douglass agreed, and the new paper was named *Frederick Douglass' Paper*. The first edition was printed in June, with the new motto, "All Rights for All!" The front page of the July 3, 1857, edition is shown here.

The Compromise of 1850 had barely been passed when a group of midwestern congressmen petitioned Congress to make Nebraska a territory. Nebraska, which was part of the Louisiana Purchase, included much of the land that now makes up the states of Nebraska, Montana, Wyoming, South Dakota, Colorado, and Kansas. Fur traders and trading post owners inhabited the area. Plans were underway for a transcontinental railroad, and midwesterners hoped it would follow a northern route through Nebraska. If the railroad was built along this route, more settlers would be attracted to the region, and the region would prosper.

Nebraska's application to become a territory set off another explosive debate over slavery and led to violence. The area was north of the 36°30' north latitude. Under the terms of the Missouri Compromise, slavery was illegal there. Unwilling to admit a territory that would become a free state, southerners in Congress refused to approve Nebraska's petition. After weeks of debate, Democratic senator Stephen A. Douglas proposed the Kansas-Nebraska Act as a compromise. The act would repeal the Missouri Compromise and divide Nebraska into two territories, Kansas and Nebraska. In each territory, the decision about slavery would be made by popular sovereignty, or a vote by the people of the territory.

The idea of repealing the Missouri Compromise met with a storm of disapproval from the abolitionists.

Without it, there would be nothing to stop slavery from spreading into the states that would be carved out of the new territories. Gerrit Smith, who had been elected to the House of Representatives from New York in 1852, gave a rousing speech against the bill. Other anti-slavery legislators echoed his wrath, but they could not generate enough votes to defeat the measure, and the Kansas-Nebraska Act was voted into law in 1854.

Popular sovereignty was not an easy answer to the question of slavery in the West. Nebraska was certain to be a free state, but the future of Kansas was unclear. Southerners wanted another slave state to join their ranks, but the settlements of rural Kansas were large-ly antislavery. The dispute became violent when groups of proslavery men from Missouri, known as bushwhackers, staged surprise attacks on antislavery settlements. Abolitionist forces retaliated in brutal skirmishes. In the end, the free-state supporters won, but the conflict over the territory's status was so violent that it became known as Bleeding Kansas.

While the conflict in Kansas raged, Frederick Douglass was busy working on another autobiography. *My Bondage and My Freedom* appeared in 1855, and sold fifteen thousand copies in two months. It was longer and

---

Previous spread: The Marais des Cygnes Massacre was the most savage encounter of the Bleeding Kansas conflict. On May 19, 1858, thirty proslavery men kidnapped eleven unarmed free-state men, led them to a clearing outside town, and attempted to execute them. Five men were killed, five were wounded, and one escaped.

more detailed than his first book and included his experiences in the antislavery movement. *My Bondage and My Freedom* began with a warm dedication to Gerrit Smith and ended with a brief summation of the goals Frederick Douglass had set for himself: "to promote the moral, social, religious, and intellectual elevation of the free colored people" and "to use my voice, my pen, or my vote, to advocate the great and primary work of the universal and unconditional emancipation of my entire race." These were ambitious goals, but Douglass felt confident that he could fulfill them.

8. Free at Last

The turmoil in Kansas highlighted the division in the abolitionist movement between those who favored ending slavery by moral persuasion and those, such as Frederick Douglass and Gerrit Smith, who thought political action was needed. Bleeding Kansas caused a further rift in the abolitionist movement between those who were against violence and those who regarded it as the only way to accomplish their goal. In the latter group, the loudest voice belonged to John Brown.

A restless man, Brown left northern New York in 1855, and went to Kansas to join the fight against slavery. In the spring of 1856, he led a vicious attack on a proslavery settlement. After fleeing Kansas, where a warrant for his arrest had been issued, Brown headed east to raise money to arm the antislavery forces. Along the way, he stopped in Rochester to see Frederick

Next page: This 1847 daguerreotype, taken by Augustus Washington, is the earliest known image of abolitionist John Brown. In 1855, Brown and five of his sons traveled to Kansas Territory to join the conflict there. At the bloody Pottawatomie Creek massacre the following year, Brown and his followers killed five unarmed men.

Douglass. During this and subsequent visits to Douglass's home in 1856 and 1858, Brown unfolded the details of his grand schemes to abolish slavery. One plan was to set up a well-guarded corridor from Virginia to Canada through which a massive number of slaves could escape to freedom. Another of Brown's schemes was to lead a slave revolt throughout the South and set up a black state in the Appalachian Mountains, complete with armed guards to hold off local militiamen, sheriffs and their deputies, and possibly the U.S. Army.

Both plans were impractical, but, by the time Brown reached the east coast, he had come up with one that had the possibility of working. He would lead a slave revolt and set up a black state in Virginia, the state with the largest number of slaves. All he needed was enough money to raise an army. Appalled by Brown's savagery in Kansas, William Lloyd Garrison refused to help, but Gerrit Smith and other wealthy white abolitionists gave Brown the necessary funds. He returned to Douglass's farmhouse to make preparations.

Douglass gave only halfhearted support to the idea. Some years earlier, he had declared that he would welcome the news that slaves had rebelled and "were engaged in spreading death and devastation." In hundreds of other speeches, however, he had stood firmly on the side of freeing blacks by peaceable means. When Brown went to Canada to enlist fugitive slaves for his insurrection, Douglass declined to join him.

Returning to the United States, Brown selected Harpers Ferry, Virginia, as the target for his military operations. In the fall of 1859, he and an army of twenty-one men captured the government arsenal at Harpers Ferry and occupied the town. When U.S. troops arrived and demanded his surrender, Brown refused. The troops took the place by storm. Ten of Brown's men died in the battle, and Brown himself was wounded. He was later put on trial and hanged for treason.

Frederick Douglass was lecturing in Philadelphia when Brown staged his raid. The incident made headlines across the country, and newspapers reported that

On December 2, 1859, John Brown climbed the steps of the scaffold in Charles Town, Virginia, and was hanged. Frederick Douglass later wrote of Brown, "His zeal in the cause of freedom was infinitely superior to mine. . . . I could live for the slave; John Brown could *die* for him."

a note from Douglass had been found among Brown's papers. The federal authorities were already searching for accomplices to the crime. Douglass knew he would be on their list of suspects. Returning to Rochester by a roundabout route, he contacted Amy and Isaac Post. Just hours before a party of marshals arrived in the city, the Posts put Douglass on a boat to Canada.

Douglass had been planning a trip to Great Britain before he heard the news of John Brown's raid. With federal marshals in pursuit, it seemed an especially good idea. He had hoped to stay abroad until the uproar died down, but, while in Britain, he received word that his youngest daughter, eleven-year-old Annie, had died. Setting aside his fear of arrest, he booked passage to America. By the time Douglass got back to Rochester, the uproar over John Brown's raid had died down. Southerners regarded Brown as a villain, but the abolitionists called him a martyr. Fearful of creating more martyrs, the government let the matter rest.

Meanwhile, the Kansas-Nebraska Act had prompted the formation of a new political party. Its members called themselves Republicans, and they were united by their opposition to the expansion of slavery into the territories. The Republicans had nominated their first presidential candidate, frontier explorer and California senator John C. Frémont, in 1856. Although Gerrit Smith had also run, Douglass had campaigned for Frémont, the only antislavery candidate who had a chance of winning. Frémont had been defeated by the Democratic candidate, James Buchanan, who had been neutral on the issue of slavery. Buchanan wanted to maintain the balance between the proslavery and antislavery forces to avoid conflict. Four years later, the Republican presidential nominee was Abraham Lincoln, and, once again, the campaign centered on the issue of slavery.

Frederick Douglass had doubts about Abraham Lincoln. Lincoln considered slavery an injustice and was opposed to extending it into the western territories, but he also supported a colony in Liberia and did not campaign for abolition. In spite of his doubts, Douglass was forced to admit that Lincoln was a far better choice than his

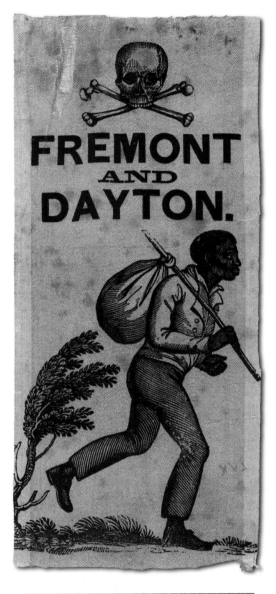

An 1856 campaign ribbon warned voters that presidential candidate John C. Frémont and his running mate, William L. Dayton, supported the rights of runaway slaves. The ribbon suggests that if Frémont and Dayton were elected, they would lead the fight to end slavery, bringing about the death of the southern way of life.

In 1858, Abraham Lincoln waged an unsuccessful campaign against Stephen A. Douglas for the Illinois seat in the Senate. Two years later, the two men ran against each other in the presidential race. John Henry Brown painted this watercolor portrait of Abraham Lincoln around 1860, during or just after his successful campaign for president.

opponent, Stephen A. Douglas, the mastermind of the Kansas-Nebraska Act. Lincoln was elected president in 1860.

Though Lincoln's positions against slavery were mild by Frederick Douglass's standards, they were too strong for the people of South Carolina, who seceded from the Union to protest Lincoln's election. In the final months of President Buchanan's term of office, six other states followed suit, and, in 1861, the Confederate States of America was formed. Buchanan left office with the country on the brink of war.

Abraham Lincoln was sworn in as president on March 4, 1861. A little more than a month later, Confederate soldiers fired on federal troops at Fort Sumter in Charleston Harbor, South Carolina. The Union troops returned fire, and the country was at war. Lincoln called it a war to preserve the Union, which indeed it was. Frederick Douglass called it a war to abolish slavery, which was also an accurate description. However, Lincoln was reluctant to make slavery the issue and potentially offend those northerners who cared little about blacks and whose support Lincoln needed to recruit an army.

Frederick Douglass had suspended publication of his debt-ridden weekly newspaper in 1860. However, he continued to make his views known in a supplement, *Frederick Douglass' Monthly*, which he had begun publishing two years earlier. Douglass's articles and lectures were unrelenting in their attacks against slavery and their demands that Lincoln make it the issue at stake in the war. The paper's circulation was too small for his articles to have much impact, but his speeches were often reported in other, larger newspapers. In one speech, "The American Apocalypse," Douglass said that when the war was finished, "not a slave should be left a slave in the returning footprints of the American army gone to put down this slaveholding rebellion. Sound policy, not less than humanity, demands the instant liberation of every slave in the rebel states."

In a Fourth of July address in New York City in 1862, Douglass attacked Lincoln directly. Referring to the president of the Confederacy, he said, "Jefferson Davis is a powerful man, but Jefferson Davis has no such power to blast the hope and break down the strong heart of this nation, as that possessed and exercised by Abraham Lincoln." Lincoln, Douglass argued, was a disappointment to the abolitionist movement.

The abolitionist movement was a powerful force. That same month, Lincoln drafted a law to emancipate the slaves and presented it to his cabinet. Secretary of State William Seward advised him not to issue it right away. The Union army had suffered one defeat after another, and it might look as if the president were desperate. Seward thought the document would have more impact if it were issued after a Union victory.

In September, at Antietam Creek in Maryland, the Union army held back a Confederate attempt to invade the North. It was the victory for which Lincoln had been waiting. He issued a preliminary proclamation shortly after the battle and announced that, unless the rebellion ceased, the document would become law on January 1, 1863. On January 1, Lincoln signed the Emancipation Proclamation, freeing all the slaves in the Confederacy, but not those in slaveholding states that had remained loyal to the Union or those in states currently under Union control. Lincoln's declaration was cautious. It was intended as a morale booster for the war-weary Unionists, not as a powerful piece of legislation. Northerners were beginning to question their

Lincoln is shown writing the Emancipation Proclamation in Ehrgott and Forbriger's lithograph, which was based on David Gilmour Blythe's painting. Lincoln's left hand rests on a Bible and a copy of the U.S. Constitution. On the floor at his feet lies a maul, a tool for splitting logs, which represents Lincoln's days as an Illinois backwoodsman.

involvement in the long war, and Lincoln hoped that the proclamation would rally their spirits and revive the war effort. To a great extent, it achieved this aim. However, many northerners were increasingly suspicious of the abolition movement. Soon after the proclamation was signed, Lincoln's home state of Illinois passed a law prohibiting future black settlement within its borders. Riots erupted in cities across the northeast as antiblack sentiment spread.

Boston's Tremont Temple is shown in this photograph from the 1860s. The temple is the building on the right with tall, arched windows. The original structure has since burned and been rebuilt.

Despite these problems, Frederick Douglass and the abolitionists embraced the Emancipation Proclamation as a declaration by the government that slavery was on its way out. On that momentous New Year's Day, Frederick Douglass took part in a vigil at Boston's Tremont Temple, where a crowd of three thousand blacks had assembled, waiting to hear that the proclamation had been signed. Around 11:00 P.M., they received the news. Douglass later recalled that, compared to the excitement of that scene, "I never saw Joy before." He went on to say that "Men, women, young and old, were up: hats and bonnets were in the air."

It was a day of celebration for every black in the country, including Frederick Douglass. His fight against slavery had at last been won.

9. War and Peace

Frederick Douglass firmly believed that blacks should take part in the Civil War and urged the Union army to accept black soldiers. The army refused. The only way blacks could fight was by joining a segregated company of volunteers. Aware that they would either be killed or sold as slaves if they were captured by Confederate forces, few blacks signed up for service. In addition, black soldiers were paid less than white soldiers and were not allowed to become officers. Determined to change the minds of young black men, Frederick Douglass issued a call for volunteers in *Frederick Douglass' Monthly* in 1863. Douglass campaigned for volunteers during a trip through western New York State, beseeching young blacks to enlist. He recruited more than one hundred men for the Fifty-Fourth Massachusetts Infantry, one of the first regiments of black troops raised in a free state. The enlistees included two of his sons, Charles and Lewis.

Douglass also went to Washington, D.C., to lobby on behalf of black soldiers. He called on a friend in the Senate, and the two men went to see Secretary of War

"Let the slaves and free colored people be called into service, and formed into a liberating army, to march into the South and raise the banner of emancipation among the slaves . . . Men of Color, To Arms!" declared Frederick Douglass. Douglass's son Lewis heard his father's call to arms. Sergeant-Major Lewis Douglass of the Fifty-Fourth Massachusetts Infantry was photographed in 1863.

Augustus Saint-Gaudens created a memorial to the men of the Fifty-Fourth Massachusetts Infantry. The original was erected in Boston Common in 1897. Saint-Gaudens made revised plaster copies of the relief, including the one shown here. Robert Gould Shaw, the white commander of the regiment, sits atop his horse in the foreground.

Edwin Stanton. The secretary promised to do what he could, but nothing was ever done.

After his visit with Stanton, Douglass went to the White House to see the president. Unlike most of the whites Douglass had met, Abraham Lincoln treated him as an equal. Douglass left the White House hopeful but uncertain that Lincoln was a man who could be counted on to look out for the interests of blacks.

In 1863, Douglass suspended publication of *Frederick Douglass' Monthly* in anticipation of being appointed as the country's first black army officer. During their meeting, Stanton had asked Douglass to help the government recruit black soldiers, indicating that Douglass would receive a commission as an officer. When his orders arrived, Douglass discovered that he was expected to serve as a civilian. It was a humiliating blow, and he politely declined the offer.

Lincoln's 1864 reelection was good news for Douglass, as was Robert E. Lee's surrender at Appomattox the following April. The Civil War had almost come to an end. Days later, however, Abraham Lincoln was assassinated. Douglass attended a memorial service in Rochester's City Hall and spoke movingly of the slain president's role as a friend to blacks.

Frederick Douglass had expected the Civil War to usher in a new era for blacks. The Thirteenth and the Fourteenth Amendments to the Constitution made slavery illegal and granted citizenship to anyone born in the United States, regardless of race. Both amendments were ratified, but there were signs that the country was not prepared to do more to improve the status of blacks. One of the government's few gestures of goodwill to former slaves was the creation of the Freedmen's Bureau. The bureau was chartered to help former slaves find homes and jobs. As did other attempts to rebuild the South during the Reconstruction, the bureau became mired in politics. Though it achieved a great deal, the Freedmen's Bureau never overcame the challenges of Reconstruction.

A group of southern blacks who had migrated to Washington, D.C., after the Civil War demanded to have the Freedmen's Bureau run by one of their own. The logical candidate was Douglass. President Andrew Johnson approached Douglass about the job. Douglass was intrigued, but he questioned whether Johnson was genuinely interested in helping former slaves. Douglass declined the president's offer, refusing to serve under a man he did not trust.

With his antislavery crusade ended, Douglass took on the challenge of universal black suffrage. He found that most of his former allies in the antislavery movement were opposed to the idea. Women abolitionists insisted that white women should be given the vote before black men, because women constituted more than half of the population.

General Ulysses S. Grant, who was elected president in 1868, would become a powerful supporter of the cause for universal male suffrage. In his inaugural address, Grant praised the proposed Fifteenth Amendment, which stated that the right to vote could not be denied on the basis of "race, color, or previous condition of servitude." The amendment was ratified the following year. In theory blacks had won the right to vote, but, in the South, corrupt voting laws kept many blacks from casting ballots.

With Grant in office, Douglass was hoping to receive a political appointment. He was honored when the president invited him to join a commission to the Dominican

On November 16, 1867, *Harper's Weekly* published this cartoon by Alfred R. Waud, a celebrated Civil War sketch artist. *The First Vote* shows three black voters casting their ballots. The laborer, the businessman, and the soldier are identifiable by their clothing.

Republic, which was then known as Santo Domingo. The president wanted to annex the Caribbean country to create a refuge for ex-slaves. The Senate had rejected the treaty of annexation, but the president refused to give up. In an effort to win public support, Grant asked four prominent men, all white except for Douglass, to visit the island and report on the Santo Domingan government's reaction to the plan. On their return, Grant invited three of the commissioners to dinner at the White House. Douglass was excluded. The country's black leaders criticized Grant for the snub. Douglass may have vented his anger in private, but he declined to criticize Grant publicly, the great Union general in the Civil War and a champion of black civil rights.

Grant was unable to persuade the Senate to approve the annexation of Santo Domingo, even though the commissioners had issued a favorable report on the plan. The president's fiercest opponent was Senator Charles Sumner of Massachusetts, who had been a staunch abolitionist. Sumner argued that blacks were Americans who deserved to be treated fairly in their own country. In other circumstances, Douglass would have agreed with Sumner, but he felt privileged to have been appointed to the commission and continued to defend Grant's policies.

In the summer of 1872, while Douglass was in Washington, D.C., he received a telegram informing him that his house in Rochester had burned to the ground. No one had been injured in the blaze, but the fire had apparently been set by an arsonist. Douglass was so disgusted that, after twenty-five years of living in Rochester, he and Anna abandoned the city and bought a house in Washington, D.C.

Two years after moving to Washington, D.C., the trustees of the Freedman's Savings and Trust Company offered Douglass the position of president, and Douglass accepted. The position gave Douglass a chance to help other blacks. The Freedman's Savings and Trust Company had been chartered by Congress to encourage fiscal responsibility among blacks. Frederick Douglass had no experience in finance and did not realize that the bank was on the verge of bankruptcy. In the summer of 1874, the trustees of the bank announced that it had failed. Hundreds of blacks

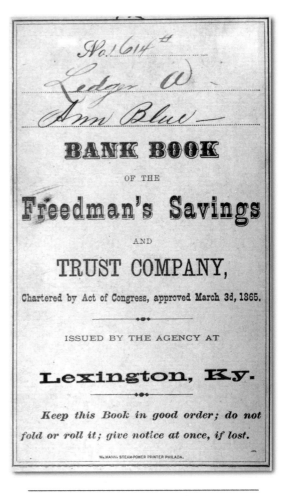

Ann Blue, a free black woman, opened an account at the Freedman's Savings and Trust Company in August 1873. She used this bankbook until the institution was dissolved in 1874.

lost their savings. Many of them blamed Frederick Douglass for their losses and demanded that he repay them. Douglass was embarrassed and apologetic, but he insisted that he too had been deceived. In a letter to Gerrit Smith, Douglass wrote, "It had been the black man's cow, but the white man's milk. Bad loans and bad management have been the end of it."

Although Frederick Douglass continued to be the most famous black man in America, he was no longer the firebrand who had led the fight against the institution of slavery. In 1878, Frederick Douglass was sixty years old and ready to settle down. He and Anna bought a fourteen-room house overlooking the Anacostia branch of the Potomac River. The house was white with a long front porch and four tall columns. It looked like a stately southern plantation. Douglass called the house Cedar Hill.

Each of the Republican presidents who succeeded Abraham Lincoln sought Douglass's advice on matters relating to blacks. They also found places for him in their administrations. In return, Douglass campaigned faithfully for Republican presidential candidates, guaranteeing them the support of countless black voters. A white man who delivered so many votes to a winning candidate would have been rewarded with an important government post. Douglass received only minor appointments. President Rutherford B. Hayes made Douglass U.S. marshal of the District of Columbia.

Frederick Douglass sits at his desk in his Cedar Hill library.
In recognition of his ongoing pursuit of scholarship,
Douglass was given the nickname the Sage of Anacostia.
A sage is a person known for his or her wisdom.

Hayes's successor, James A. Garfield, made Douglass the District's recorder of deeds. Although neither position gave Douglass much power, there was consolation in the fact that they provided him with opportunities to hire blacks for government jobs.

10. Final Days

In 1881, Frederick Douglass published his third auto-biography, *Life and Times of Frederick Douglass*. In this version, he brought his life story up to date with a commentary on the Civil War and its outcome. He was concerned that America's history of slavery was in danger of being forgotten, even by blacks, and he warned his readers not to forget their shared past. The book sold few copies. Apparently, Americans did not want to be reminded of this shameful episode in their national history.

Slavery was an experience that Douglass could never forget. His experiences as a slave remained vivid in his mind throughout adulthood. Still, he felt a deep affection for his native state, Maryland. In 1877, Douglass had returned to the Eastern Shore. He had many relatives still living in St. Michael's, but his first visit had been to his former master, Thomas Auld.

Opposite: Frederick Douglass was living proof that "neither slavery, stripes, imprisonment, or proscription, need extinguish self-respect, crush manly ambition, or paralyze effort." These words, from his 1881 biography, were a call to action directed at all black Americans. Here he is shown in a photograph taken by George K. Warren around 1879.

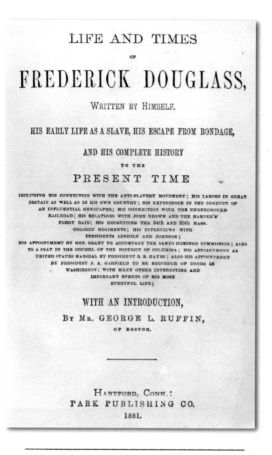

LIFE AND TIMES

OF

FREDERICK DOUGLASS,

WRITTEN BY HIMSELF.

HIS EARLY LIFE AS A SLAVE, HIS ESCAPE FROM BONDAGE,

AND HIS COMPLETE HISTORY

TO THE

PRESENT TIME

INCLUDING HIS CONNECTION WITH THE ANTI-SLAVERY MOVEMENT; HIS LABORS IN GREAT BRITAIN AS WELL AS IN HIS OWN COUNTRY; HIS EXPERIENCE IN THE CONDUCT OF AN INFLUENTIAL NEWSPAPER; HIS CONNECTION WITH THE UNDERGROUND RAILROAD; HIS RELATIONS WITH JOHN BROWN AND THE HARPER'S FERRY RAID; HIS RECRUITING THE 54th AND 55th MASS. COLORED REGIMENTS; HIS INTERVIEWS WITH PRESIDENTS LINCOLN AND JOHNSON; HIS APPOINTMENT BY GEN. GRANT TO ACCOMPANY THE SANTO DOMINGO COMMISSION; ALSO TO A SEAT IN THE COUNCIL OF THE DISTRICT OF COLUMBIA; HIS APPOINTMENT AS UNITED STATES MARSHAL BY PRESIDENT R. B. HAYES; ALSO HIS APPOINTMENT BY PRESIDENT J. A. GARFIELD TO BE RECORDER OF DEEDS IN WASHINGTON; WITH MANY OTHER INTERESTING AND IMPORTANT EVENTS OF HIS MOST EVENTFUL LIFE;

WITH AN INTRODUCTION,

BY MR. GEORGE L. RUFFIN,

OF BOSTON.

HARTFORD, CONN.:
PARK PUBLISHING CO.
1881.

"The time is at hand when the last American slave, and the last American slaveholder will disappear behind the curtain which separates the living from the dead . . . My part has been to tell the story of the slave," wrote Frederick Douglass at the end of his 1881 biography.

Douglass had found Auld on his deathbed. They had greeted each other warmly and wept. Auld had been pleased and proud that Frederick had become a famous man. He had forgiven Douglass for the harsh remarks about Auld that had appeared in Douglass's books and speeches. Frederick Douglass, in turn, had been grateful to Auld for sending him to Baltimore to learn the trade of a caulker. Then the two men had parted on friendly terms.

In 1882, Frederick Douglass had to endure the loss of his wife, Anna, who suffered a stroke and died. Their marriage had not been a close one. Douglass was often away from home, and Anna had never learned to read and did not share his intellectual interests. Still, Douglass could not forget that it was Anna who had given him the money to escape from slavery. She had stood in the background, managing their home and raising their children, while he devoted his attention to the abolitionist cause.

Douglass was deeply depressed after Anna's death. His energy and good spirits gradually returned, however, and he fell in love with forty-five-year-old Helen Pitts. Douglass and Pitts met often at women's rights meetings and saw each other even more frequently when she took a job as a clerk in Douglass's office.

Helen Pitts was white, and her interracial relationship with Douglass caused an uproar in both their families. Douglass's daughter, Rosetta, was outspoken in her opposition to the match. His sons and daughters-in-law were equally negative. Helen Pitts's mother and sisters were more understanding, but her father, Gideon Pitts, was not. He had once been a staunch abolitionist. After the war, however, as had many former abolitionists, Pitts had lost his enthusiasm for racial equality. In spite of the objections of their families, Frederick Douglass and Helen Pitts were married on January 24, 1884.

After resigning as recorder of deeds in 1886, Douglass used his newly acquired leisure to travel abroad, where he introduced his second wife to his old friends in Great Britain and took her on a tour that included France, Italy, Greece, and Egypt.

Three years later, Republican Benjamin Harrison was in the White House. Douglass hoped to be offered his former position as recorder of deeds. Instead Harrison asked

The Pitts family traced its ancestry to *Mayflower* passengers John Alden and Priscilla Mullins, and to former U.S. presidents John Adams and John Quincy Adams. Helen Pitts was raised among political activists and was educated at Mount Holyoke Seminary. This photograph was taken by J. H. Kent in Rochester, New York.

him to take a more impressive appointment as minist[er]
resident and consul general to Haiti. Formerly a Fren[ch]
possession, Haiti had won its independence in 1804.

The Douglasses arrived in Port-au-Prince, Haiti, i[n]
October 1889, and the new minister presented his cre-
dentials to President Louis Mondestin Florvil Hyppolite.
The Douglasses found it a welcome change to be in a
country where his race was not an issue. Virtually the
entire population could trace its ancestors back to the
African slaves who had been brought to the island by the
French. Douglass enjoyed good relations with Hyppolite.
Their relations became strained only when U.S. secretary of state James G. Blaine asked Douglass to negoti-
ate an agreement that would allow U.S. Navy ships to
use one of Haiti's largest ports as a fueling station.

Skeptical of Douglass's skills as a negotiator and
convinced that he was too sympathetic to the Haitians,
Blaine sent an American admiral to take over the nego-
tiations. The admiral, too, was unsuccessful. Irritated
at the state department, Douglass returned to the
United States, and resigned in the summer of 1891.

Frederick Douglass continued to be a hero to blacks,
but his accomplishments were gradually receding into
history. Former abolitionists were now working for
other social reforms, such as temperance and women's
suffrage, and the rest of the country was preoccupied
with other issues. Many Americans, in fact, resented
blacks and blamed them for the Civil War.

A flash of Douglass's old fire returned when he delivered an address at the World's Columbian Exposition in Chicago in 1893. The president of Haiti had appointed Douglass commissioner of the Haitian pavilion, which featured exhibits about the country and its people, but he was one of the few blacks to play a major role in the event. Worse yet, there was not a single exhibit that focused on black accomplishments. To make up for the slight, Douglass urged the exposition's organizers to hold a Colored People's Day during the exposition. He envisioned a celebration of black poets, musicians, and other artists. Instead the organizers

The World's Columbian Exposition was held in Chicago, Illinois, in the summer of 1893. It was intended as a celebration of American independence, commerce, and creativity and as an introduction to the cultures of the world. More than 27 million people, or almost one out of every four people living in the United States at the time, visited the fairground, a portion of which is shown here.

turned it into a tasteless joke by setting up watermelon stands around the exposition grounds. Watermelons had long been used by cartoonists in caricatures of crude, poorly-educated blacks. When word of this stereotypical representation of African American culture became public, many blacks boycotted the event.

At Festival Hall that afternoon, Frederick Douglass was scheduled to deliver the speech "The Race Problem in America." As he put on his glasses and started to read from the papers in his hands, a group of white men at the back of the hall interrupted him with jeers. Douglass stopped. His voice faltered for an instant. Then he threw down his papers, took off his glasses, and launched into an oration that was as powerful as any he had ever given. His voice drowned out the hecklers. "Men talk of the Negro problem," he thundered. "There is no Negro problem. The problem is whether the American people have loyalty enough, honor enough, patriotism enough to live up to their own Constitution." The speech lasted for an hour and turned Colored People's Day into a rousing triumph for black Americans.

When the World's Columbian Exposition closed in the fall of 1893, Douglass turned his attention to the crusade against lynching, led by a young black woman from Memphis, Tennessee, named Ida B. Wells. Douglass continued to accept speaking engagements, but his schedule was much less full than it had been in the past.

On February 20, 1895, Frederick Douglass addressed a meeting of the National Council of Women in Washington, D.C. He returned to Cedar Hill at midday, and, as he was describing the meeting to Helen, he crumpled to the floor, suffering from a stroke. He died within minutes.

Thousands of mourners lined up to pay their respects at Washington D.C.'s Metropolitan African

Methodist Episcopal Church, after which Douglass's body was taken to Rochester, where it was formally displayed at City Hall. After another crowded service in Rochester's Central Church, Frederick Douglass was buried in Mount Hope Cemetery beside his first wife, Anna, and their daughter, Annie.

Frederick Douglass has earned a place in American history as one of the country's first black activists. His accomplishments

A memorial to Frederick Douglass was dedicated in October 1996, in front of the New Bedford, Massachusetts, City Hall. The plaque bears a quote from Douglass: "For my part, I should prefer death to hopeless bondage."

are commemorated in the Frederick Douglass Museum and Cultural Center in Rochester, New York. His home in Washington, D.C., is a national historic site. His books and speeches have been reprinted and are studied in schools and colleges.

With Douglass's death, the civil rights movement went into decline. It was not until the 1950s that a new generation of black leaders, led by the Reverend Martin Luther King Jr., among others, took up the fight with determination equal to that of Frederick Douglass. The former slave would have been pleased to see how much progress has been made in the intervening years, but he would also be the first to point out that still more remains to be done.

Timeline

1818   Frederick Augustus Washington Bailey is born on an unknown date in February.

1824   Frederick is taken to live at Aaron Anthony's home on the Lloyd plantation.

1826   In March, Frederick is sent to live with Hugh and Sophia Auld in Baltimore.

1833   In March, Frederick is sent back to the Eastern Shore to live with Thomas and Rowena Auld in St. Michael's.

1834   On January 1, Frederick is hired out to work on Edward Covey's farm.

1836   He makes his first attempt to escape, is caught, and is sent back to Baltimore.

1838   In September, Frederick escapes to the North.

Anna Murray and Frederick are married in New York. They settle in New Bedford, Massachusetts, and change their last name to Douglass.

1839   The Douglasses' first child, Rosetta, is born on June 24.

1840   The Douglasses' son Lewis Henry is born on October 9.

1841   Douglass becomes a speaker for the Massachusetts Anti-Slavery Society.

1842   Douglass becomes a speaker for the American Anti-Slavery Society.

The Douglasses' second son, Frederick, is born on March 3.

1844   The Douglasses' third son, Charles Remond, is born on October 21.

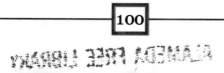

1845	*The Narrative of the Life of Frederick Douglass, an American Slave, Written by Himself* is published.
	Douglass goes on a lecture tour of Great Britain.
1846	On December 12, Douglass becomes legally free.
1847	Douglass publishes the first issue of the *North Star* in Rochester, New York.
1848	Douglass attends the first women's rights convention in Seneca Falls, New York.
1849	The Douglasses' daughter Annie is born on March 22.
	Julia Griffiths arrives in Rochester to help Douglass publish the *North Star*.
1851	Douglass changes the name of the *North Star* to *Frederick Douglass' Paper*.
	Douglass publicly disagrees with William Lloyd Garrison that the Constitution is a proslavery document.
1854	Douglass breaks off his friendship with William Lloyd Garrison and stops attending meetings of the American Anti-Slavery Society.
1855	Douglass publishes his second autobiography, *My Bondage and My Freedom*.
1858	Douglass begins publishing *Frederick Douglass' Monthly* as a supplement to his weekly newspaper.
1859	Douglass is suspected of being an accomplice to John Brown's raid on Harpers Ferry, Virginia.
	Douglass embarks on a lecture tour of England.
1860	Douglass stops publishing *Frederick Douglass' Paper*.
1863	On New Year's Day, Douglass celebrates the signing of the Emancipation Proclamation.
	Douglass becomes a recruiting agent for the Fifty-Fourth

Massachusetts Infantry.

Douglass suspends publication of *Frederick Douglass' Monthly*.

1867   Douglass receives an indirect offer to become head of the Freedmen's Bureau, which he declines.

1871   President Ulysses S. Grant appoints Douglass to a commission to investigate the possibility of annexing Santo Domingo.

1874   In March, Douglass becomes president of the Freedman's Savings and Trust Company, which closes on July 1.

1877   Douglass is appointed U.S. marshal for the District of Columbia by President Rutherford B. Hayes.

Douglass returns to St. Michael's for a reunion with Thomas Auld.

1878   Douglass purchases Cedar Hill.

1881   President James A. Garfield appoints Douglass recorder of deeds for the District of Columbia.

Douglass publishes his third autobiography, *Life and Times of Frederick Douglass*, which sells very few copies.

1882   Anna Murray Douglass dies on August 4.

1884   Douglass marries Helen Pitts on January 24.

1886   Douglass resigns as recorder of deeds, and he and his wife travel abroad.

1889   On July 1, Douglass is appointed minister resident and consul general to Haiti by President Benjamin Harrison.

1891   On July 30, Douglass resigns his position in Haiti and returns to Washington.

1895   Frederick Douglass dies on February 20.

Glossary

abuse (uh-BYOOS) To treat in a harmful way.

accomplices (uh-KOM-plis-ez) People who help another in a crime or wrongdoing.

accurate (A-kyuh-rit) Exactly right.

advocate (AD-vuh-kayt) To speak in favor of.

annihilate (uh-NY-uh-layt) To cause to cease to exist.

apprentice (uh-PREN-tis) An individual who works without pay in order to learn a skill or a craft.

arsonist (AR-sun-ist) A person who starts fires on purpose.

autobiography (aw-toh-by-AH-gruh-fee) The story of a person's life written by that person.

ballot (BA-lut) A piece of paper used in voting.

bankruptcy (BANK-rup-see) Official declaration by a person or a business of an inability to pay money that is owed, resulting in legal proceedings and loss of property.

barbarity (bar-BAR-uh-tee) Extreme cruelty.

campaign (kam-PAYN) A plan to achieve a specific result, such as to win an election.

certify (SUR-tih-fy) To state in writing that something is true.

counterfeit (KOWN-tur-fit) To copy something in order to deceive.

dissolution (dih-suh-LOO-shun) The undoing or breaking of a bond.

firebrand (FYR-brand) Someone who causes unrest.

forged (FORJD) To have written something that is false.

husks (HUSKS) The dry, external covering of various fruits, plants, and seeds.

hypocrisy (hih-PAH-kruh-see) Pretending to have high principles, beliefs, or feelings.

impostor (im-POS-ter) A person who assumes a different character or name to deceive others.

inequities (ih-NEH-kwuh-teez) Unfair circumstances or proceedings.

insurrection (in-suh-REK-shun) Rebelling against someone's control, usually with weapons.

lynch (LINCH) To kill a person by mob action and without legal authority.

martyr (MAR-ter) Someone who dies or is killed for a cause or a principle.

militant (MIH-luh-tent) Strict.

narrative (NAR-uh-tiv) A story.

neutral (NOO-trul) On neither side of an argument or a war.

orator (OR-uh-tur) A skilled public speaker.

protracted (proh-TRAKT-ed) Delayed.

pummel (PUH-mul) To beat with one's fists.

ratified (RA-tih-fyd) To have been approved officially.

Reconstruction (ree-kun-STRUK-shun) A period in U.S. history after the Civil War (1865–1877) when the Confederate states attempted to rebuild their economies.

regiment (REH-jih-ment) A military unit.

stronghold (STRONG-hohld) A well-guarded place.

switches (SWICH-ez) Slender, flexible whips, rods, or twigs.

testimony (TES-tuh-moh-nee) Statements made by witnesses under oath.

vigils (VIH-jilz) Watching; maintaining wakefulness during the usual hours of sleep.

wharves (WORVZ) Large docks or piers, where ships load and unload goods and people.

Additional Resources

To learn more about Frederick Douglass, check out the following books and Web sites:

Books

Davidson, Margaret. *Frederick Douglass Fights for Freedom*. New York: Four Winds Press, 1968.

Douglass, Frederick. *Frederick Douglass in His Own Words*. Edited by Milton Meltzer. New York: Harcourt Brace and Company, 1995.

Douglass, Frederick. *Life and Times of Frederick Douglass*. Adapted by Barbara Ritchie. New York: Thomas Y. Crowell Company, 1966.

Russell, Sharman Apt. *Frederick Douglass*. New York: Chelsea House Publishers, 1988.

Web Sites

Due to the changing nature of Internet links, PowerPlus Books has developed an online list of Web sites related to the subject of this book. This site is updated regularly. Please use this link to access the list: www.powerkidslinks.com/lalt/fdouglas/

Bibliography

Douglass, Frederick. *Autobiographies*. Reprint, ed. Henry Louis Gates Jr. New York: The Library of America, 1994.

Douglass, Frederick. *My Bondage and My Freedom*. 1855. Reprint, with an introduction by Philip S. Foner. New York: Dover Publications, Inc., 1969.

Douglass, Frederick. *Narrative of the Life of Frederick Douglass, an American Slave, written by Himself*. Edited by Benjamin Quarles. 1845, Reprint. Cambridge, Massachusetts: The Belknap Press of Harvard University Press, 1960.

Fogel, Robert William, and Stanley L. Engerman. *Time on the Cross: The Economics of American Negro Slavery*. Boston: Little, Brown and Company, 1974.

Huggins, Nathan Irvin. *Slave and Citizen: The Life of Frederick Douglass*. Boston: Little, Brown and Company, 1980.

Martin, Waldo E. *The Mind of Frederick Douglass*. Chapel Hill, North Carolina: The University of North Carolina Press, 1984.

McFeely, William S. *Frederick Douglass*. New York: W. W. Norton & Company, 1991.

Preston, Dickson J. *Young Frederick Douglass: The Maryland Years*. Baltimore: Johns Hopkins University Press, 1980.

Index

About the Author

Alice Fleming is the author of more than thirty books for adults and young people. One of her favorite subjects is American history, which has led her to write about a wide variety of famous Americans, including George Washington, P. T. Barnum, Ida Tarbell, and Senator Margaret Chase Smith. Ms. Fleming lives in New York City with her husband, novelist and historian Thomas Fleming.

Primary Sources

Cover. *Frederick Douglass*, lithograph, between 1870–1890, Library of Congress Prints and Photographs Division. **Page 4**. *Frederick Douglass*, photograph, circa 1840, Bettmann/Corbis. **Page 7**. Slaves supervised by an overseer, watercolor on paper, 1798, Benjamin Henry Latrobe, the Maryland Historical Society, Baltimore, Maryland. **Page 13**. Overseer Austin Gore shooting a slave as the slave attempts to escape, the Schomburg Center. **Page 19**. African-American Methodists holding a meeting in Philadelphia, watercolor and pen and ink on paper, circa 1811–1813, John Lewis Krimmel, the Metropolitan Museum of Art. **Page 21**. Nat Turner preaching in the forest, hand-colored engraving, 19th century, the Granger Collection, New York. **Page 23**. African-Americans stacking wheat near Culpeper Courthouse, Virginia, September 26, 1863, Edwin Forbes, Library of Congress Prints and Photographs. **Page 26**. Newspaper notice, paid for by William Burke, advertising reward for the capture of a runaway slave, September 3, 1838, Library of Congress, Rare Books and Special Collections Division. **Page 30**. The Smith and Dimon Shipyard in New York City, 1833, James Pringle, Library of Congress Prints and Photographs. **Page 32**. *Anna Murray Douglass*, photograph, undated, photographer unkown, Frederick Douglass National Historic Site. **Page 35**. Seaman's protection certificate for Samuel Fox, August 12, 1854, Black History Collection, Library of Congress Rare Book and Special Collection Division. **Page 37**. *William Lloyd Garrison*, 1833, Nathaniel Jocelyn, National Portrait Gallery, Smithsonian Institution/Art Resource. **Page 42**. *Elizabeth Cady Stanton*, photograph, circa 19th century, Bettmann/Corbis. **Page 43**. *Negro expulsion from railway car, Philadelphia*, wood engraving, September 27, 1856, appeared in the *Illustrated London News*, Library of Congress. **Page 46**. *Narrative of the Life of Frederick Douglass, an American Slave. Written by himself*, published in Boston at the Anti Slavery Office, 1845, Library of Congress. **Page 50**. *Amy Post*, photograph, 19th century, the Department of Rare Books and Special Collections, University of Rochester Libraries. **Page 51**. *Gerrit Smith*, circa 1864–74, Cornell University. **Page 52**. The *North Star*, edition of

June 2, 1848, Library of Congress Rare Book and Special Collections Division. **Page 53**. *Our roll of honor, signatures to the "Declaration of Sentiments,"* July 19–20, 1848, recorded by Eizabeth Cady Stanton, Library of Congress Rare Book and Special Collections Division. **Page 56**. Fugitive Slave Law Convention, Cazenovia, New York, daguerreotype, August 22, 1850, Ezra Greenleaf Weld, Getty Museum. **Pages 58–59**. Map of the United States, the British provinces, and Mexico, 1849, J. H. Colton, Library of Congress Geography and Map Division. **Page 62**. *Frederick Douglass' Paper*, edition of August 1, 1857, Courtesy of the Department of Rare Books and Special Collections, University of Rochester Libraries. **Pages 64–65**. Marais Des Cygnes, Kansas, Massacre, circa 1858, Hulton/Archive by Getty Images. **Page 69**. *John Brown*, daguerreotype, circa 1847, Augustus Washington, National Portrait Gallery, Smithsonian Institution/Art Resource, NY. Washington was the son of a former slave. **Page 71**. John Brown's Execution, circa 1859, Corbis. **Page 73**. Anti-Fremont campaign ribbon, 1856, David J. & Janice L. Frent Collection/Corbis. **Page 74**. *Abraham Lincoln*, ambrotype, October 11, 1858, William Judkins Thomson, National Portrait Gallery, Smithsonian Institution/Art Resource. **Page 77**. *President Lincoln Writing the Proclamation of Freedom, January 1, 1863*, lithograph, 1864, Ehrgott and Forbriger, Library of Congress. **Page 78**. Boston's Tremont Street, photograph, circa 1860, the Bostonian Society. **Page 81**. *Lewis Douglass*, photograph, Howard University Archive. **Page 85**. *The First Vote*, engraving, published in *Harper's Weekly* on November 16, 1867, Alfred R. Waud, Hulton Archive. **Page 87**. Account book for the Freedman's Savings and Trust Company for an account held by Ann Blue, August 1873, National Archives and Records Administration. **Page 89**. *Frederick Douglass*, photogrpah taken at Cedar Hill, Frederick Douglass National Historic Site. **Page 91**. *Frederick Douglass*, photograph, George K. Warren, Corbis. **Page 92**. *Life and Times of Frederick Douglass, Written by Himself*, published 1881, by Park Publishing Co., Schomburg Center. **Page 94**. *Helen Pitts Douglass*, sepia-toned photograph, J. H. Kent, Frederick Douglass National Historic Site. **Page 96**. World's Columbian Exposition, Chicago, Illinois, photograph, 1893, Frances Benjamin Johnston, Library of Congress Prints and Photographs Division.

Credits

Photo Credits

Cover (portrait), pp. 15, 23, 30, 34, 77, 96 Library of Congress Prints and Photographs Division; cover (background image), pp. 26, 46 Library of Congress, Rare Book and Special Collections Division; pp. 4, 42 © Bettmann/CORBIS; p. 7 The Maryland Historical Society, Baltimore, Maryland; pp. 11, 58–59 Library of Congress Geography and Map Division; p. 13, 92 Manuscripts, Archives and Rare Books Division, The Schomburg Center for Research in Black Culture, NYPL; p. 19 The Metropolitan Museum of Art, Rogers Fund, 1942 (42.95.19) Photograph © 1985 The Metropolitan Museum of Art; p. 21 The Granger Collection, New York; pp. 32, 49, 89, 94 Frederick Douglass National Historical Site; p. 35 Library of Congress Black History Collection, Manuscript Division; p. 37 National Portrait Gallery, Smithsonian Institution, Bequest of Garrison Norton/Art Resource, NY; p. 43 Library of Congress; pp. 50, 62 Images courtesy of the Department of Rare Books & Special Collections, University of Rochester Libraries; p. 51 Cornell University; p. 52 Library of Congress Serial and Government Publications Division; p. 53 Library of Congress Manuscript Division; p. 56 © The J. Paul Getty Museum; pp. 64–65, 85 Hulton/Archive by Getty Images; pp. 69, 74 National Portrait Gallery, Smithsonian Institution/Art Resource, NY; pp. 71, 91 © CORBIS; p. 73 © David J. & Janice L. Frent Collection/CORBIS; p. 78 The Bostonian Society; p. 81 Howard University Archives Moorland Springarn Research Center; p. 82 courtesy U.S. Department of the Interior, National Park Service, Saint-Gaudens National Historic Site, Cornish, N.H.; p. 87 National Archives and Records Administration; p. 98 Photograph by Tim Sylvia.

Project Editor
Gillian Houghton

Series Design
Laura Murawski

Layout Design
Corinne L. Jacob

Photo Researcher
Jeffrey Wendt